W9-ARW-147

Ultimate Speed-Reading

Second Edition

Arthur H. Bell, Ph.D. ◆ H. Bernard Wechsler

BARRON'S

About the Authors

Dr. Arthur H. Bell is a professor of management communication and director of communication programs at the Masagung Graduate School of Management, University of San Francisco. He is the author of many books, including Barron's *Business Success: Winning with Difficult People*. H. Bernard Wechsler, an original partner in the Evelyn Wood Speed-Reading Program, is a senior educational director of the Speedlearning Institute and a consultant to the Learning Annex's audio and visual reading program.

Copyright © 2013, 2006 by Barron's Educational Series, Inc.

All rights reserved.

No part of this book may be reproduced or distributed in any form or by any means without the written permission of the copyright owner.

All inquiries should be addressed to:
Barron's Educational Series, Inc.
250 Wireless Boulevard
Hauppauge, NY 11788
www.barronseduc.com

ISBN: 978-1-4380-0165-4

Library of Congress Catalog Card Number 2012956242

Printed in China
9 8 7 6 5 4 3 2 1

Contents

◆

Acknowledgments

◆

Dr. Bell would like to thank his colleagues in academia and business for their generous insights, stories, questions, experiences, and suggestions that contributed to this book. On the academic side, he owes deep gratitude to his friends and colleagues at Harvard University, Georgetown University, the University of Southern California, the Naval Postgraduate School, and the University of San Francisco. In his business life and consulting work, he is equally grateful to corporate leaders, executives, managers, and employees at all levels in the following organizations for teaching him about the real-world communication needs of practicing professionals: Citibank, TRW, Lockheed Martin, Cost Plus World Market, Apple Computer, IBM, Wells Fargo Bank, the U.S. Navy, the U.S. Department of State, British Telecommunications, Deutsche Telekom, Johnson & Johnson, American Stores, Global Technologies, Starkist, Cushman & Wakefield, Charles Schwab, Santa Fe Railway, and many other organizations with whom he has consulted. On a personal level, he extends his thanks beyond measure to his wife and partner, Dr. Dayle Smith, for having the patience to read his work and the graceful courage to criticize it. Both authors also express sincere gratitude to Marcy Rosenbaum and the entire book editing and production staff at Barron's Educational Series, Inc. Their expertise and commitment have contributed immeasurably to the second edition of this book.

Finally, the authors would like to thank Al Tuve, President of the American Speed-Reading Corporation, for his helpful comments on an earlier draft of the book and the staff of Barron's Educational Series, Inc., for their help in turning the manuscript into a finished book.

Preface

◆

If you are in a hurry to read more quickly, you no doubt will appreciate a succinct preface so that you can get right to the core lessons of this book. We, the authors, have arranged in these chapters a dozen or so proven techniques to increase your reading speed many times over while also significantly improving your comprehension and retention.

What's required of you, other than a careful reading of this book? We ask that you devote thirty minutes per day for a period of three weeks to practice, practice, practice the techniques and strategies revealed here. Toward that end, we have devoted approximately one-third of the book to exercises. First, you will find brief Time Out exercises throughout the chapters. These exercises are short reading workouts that give you a chance to try a given skill or technique right on the spot before moving on with your reading. This second edition focuses many exercises and considerable instruction on reading e-mail and text messages, since these forms of writing have become so prevalent in our professional and personal lives. Second, we provide extensive Practice Sessions at the ends of chapters. These more lengthy exercises require you to read a passage, and then take a quick comprehension quiz to make sure your understanding is keeping pace with your increased rates of reading speed. Finally, chapters conclude with Free Reading. After all, your goal must be to apply speed-reading techniques to *your* chosen books, articles, and other reading matter, not ours. Free Reading assignments ask you to select a favorite novel or other pleasurable reading matter and then to apply the lessons of the chapters to that reading experience.

The daily work on your part need not feel burdensome. In most cases, you will be reading what you want—but with the advantage of using new patterns of eye movement and new ways of thinking to vastly accelerate your reading speed and enhance comprehension.

Before turning you loose on lessons that may well change your professional and personal life in remarkable ways, we want to congratulate you for taking on the challenge of new learning. It is always easier to settle for the status quo when it comes to familiar habits, including reading habits. You have selected a learning path that U.S. presidents, CEOs, astronauts, managers, and all manner of other professionals have successfully taken before you. We are confident that the learning journey we have set forth for you in this book will take you quickly and happily to your desired destination as a skilled speed-reader. Let's begin!

Arthur H. Bell, Ph.D. and
H. Bernard Wechsler

Chapter 1

The Speed-Reading Adventure Begins

◆

"One's feelings ought all to be distilled into action and into actions that bring results."
—*Florence Nightingale*
(1820–1910)

THIS CHAPTER ANSWERS FOUR QUESTIONS:

◆ Why learn to speed-read? What are the career disadvantages of remaining an "average" reader?

◆ How did we each acquire our basic slow-go reading habits—and how can they be unlearned?

◆ What is the "word blizzard" and how does it impact virtually every professional?

◆ What are the key benefits of learning to speed-read?

Why learn to speed-read? If you are holding this book in hand or browsing its contents online, you probably have a ready answer to that question: "Because I want to get my work done more quickly and have time for others things, including some pleasure reading." Or your focus may be on increasing the amount of your reading: "I read too little—maybe just one or two books a year—because it takes me so long to read even a few pages." For most of us, reading more and comprehending more (by choice or necessity) involves "getting through" an ever-increasing number of e-mails and text messages. Throughout this second edition, techniques are taught for speeding your reading of e-mails and on-screen text in all its forms. This book is designed to help you achieve your reading goals, professional and personal, in a matter of hours, not months.

We won't waste a moment in getting you right to the techniques and practice exercises that will increase your reading speed many times over. Let's take a few pages, however, to glimpse the "big picture" involved in speed-reading before we move to the nitty-gritty of specific lessons. A broad view of the subject will serve not only to motivate you but also to help you conceive of creative applications for speed-reading in your work group, small business, or corporate environment.

You will find that "big picture thinking" is crucial to the entire enterprise of learning to speed-read. The more you know about context (where you have been on a page and where you are headed), the more you can guess in advance what the author will write next. That ability to see "around the next corner" gives you a significant head start on readers who are trying to make sense of a printed line word by word.

TYPICAL COMPLAINTS OF AVERAGE READERS

Few of us are eager to describe our reading abilities as "average." Yet the great majority of us—perhaps as many as 90 percent of the readers of this book—read factual material (of the sort found in business reports, news articles, e-mails, text messages, blogs, search-engine texts, downloaded books, and print as well as online magazine features) at a plodding rate of four or five minutes per page. At this rate it takes an hour to read a twelve- to fifteen-page business document. It is hardly surprising that a recent Gallup Poll revealed that the average American adult reads only one book per year.

Heaven knows we would like to read books and other documents more quickly, without sacrificing comprehension. What holds us back? Here are seven typical complaints from average readers as they describe what slows them down in the reading process. See if one or more of these complaints is your own:

◆ "I start reading with energy and focus. But after a page or so I find my mind wandering. I finish a paragraph only to realize that I didn't really grasp what it was saying. So I spend a lot of my reading time going back and reading stuff twice." (Studies in fact show that, on average, college graduates backtrack about twenty times per page in their reading.)

◆ "It's a little embarrassing to admit, but I can almost feel my lips moving when I read anything more difficult than paperback fiction. I end up reading at about the same pace that I would speak the sentences."

◆ "My problem is impatience. I kind of get the idea of what a paragraph is about from the first sentence and then skip on to other passages that catch my eye in the paragraph. But it's a hit-and-miss process. Many times I discover that I haven't correctly understood what the writer was trying to say."

◆ "My mind always seems to be a step behind my eyes when I read. I get to the end of a sentence with my eyes and realize that I'm still only halfway through the sentence in terms of making sense of it. So I tend to stop and let my eyes drift back to midsentence as a way of catching up."

◆ "Maybe there is something wrong with my eyes. I just don't track very well, especially when reading long documents in a small font. I focus on the first words in the line, but then my eyes may jump to the first words in the next line instead of looking at the end of the line."

◆ "I have what my wife calls the 'yada-yada' problem when I read. I think I know what the writer is going to say, so I don't pay much attention to the individual sentences. I just kind of skim the document."

◆ "I have an attitude problem. Within a few sentences when reading a document, I often develop negative feelings toward the writer. Inside I'm saying, 'What a blowhard! This guy takes twenty words to express a simple idea.' The rest of the reading experience is like a wrestling match as I struggle against the way the writer presents his or her material."

THE SOURCE OF OUR READING HABITS

In school most of us were told what to read but not how to read. We were very much on our own in developing methods for translating black marks on a white page into meaningful sentences. If we were given any advice on how to read, we were counseled to "read carefully," to "make sure we pay attention to each word," and to "remember what we read." As illustrated by the readers' experiences just cited, our approaches to reading often turned out to be inefficient and frustrating.

Pain in this case didn't lead to gain. We persisted (sometimes for decades) in our slow reading habits, for lack of guidance on better ways of proceeding. In many cases our reading behaviors have become "invisible" to us. We realize that we read too slowly and perhaps with too little comprehension and retention—but we can't identify exactly what we're doing wrong.

Time Out

To approach the important problem of what goes wrong with our reading, take a moment to read the following passage. In addition to focusing on what the passage says, be aware of what your eyes and mind are doing as you proceed through this brief reading experience. Then, in the space provided, jot down what you discovered about how you read.

"At heart, Management by Objectives (MBO) involves joint goal setting between a superior and a subordinate. The manager or supervisor wants to distribute necessary work in such a way that employees are challenged to use their individual skills without feeling overwhelmed or underutilized. The employees, similarly, want to negotiate an agreed-upon set of goals at which they can succeed with reasonable effort. Once clear goals have been established, the exact specification of tasks is often left to the employee, subject to managerial review. If the goal, for example, is the development of a site plan for a building, the company architect accepting that goal will not be told point-for-point how to go about developing the site plan. The architect's expertise is relied upon and taken for granted. When goals have been negotiated, they become the primary standard by which employee effectiveness is measured. In our earlier example, a company architect working toward the goal of developing a site plan agrees to produce approved renderings of that plan by a certain date. If that goal is accomplished on or before the deadline, the architect deserves company rewards (typically in the form of a raise or promotion). If not, the architect may be in line for a variety of company demerits, including salary reduction, demotion, or termination."

In the following space, write down what you observed about your own way of reading (including eye movements, back-tracking, skipping ahead, and so forth):

I read line by line from beginning to end
I will re-read if I dont understand the 1st
sentence

This information about your own reading habits will become quite useful as you learn new techniques and strategies for speed-reading in coming chapters.

A WORD ABOUT SPEED AND COMPREHENSION

Let's take a moment early on to dispel two urban myths. First, there is the mistaken idea that "speed-readers don't really understand what they're reading." If you have witnessed an adept speed-reader enjoying a 400-page novel in forty-five minutes or less instead of several hours or days, you too may have wondered if the reader is "getting anything" or is just reading for the bare bones of the plot.

On every comprehension test available, speed-readers score significantly higher (15 to 20 percent is typical) than their previous scores before they learned to speed-read. Memory tests, both short- and long-term, yield the same positive results.

A second urban myth has it that "speed-readers are just showing off, trying to impress others with how fast they can turn the pages." Not so. Speed-readers are involved in their reading experience and, in most cases, enjoying it. They are simply enjoying it in less time than it takes average readers. According to a statistic frequently quoted by several well-known speed-reading institutes and consultants, a tenfold increase in reading speed can be expected over initial reading rates by students who see the program through.

Speed, in fact, is quickly forgotten by trained speed-readers, who are usually much too busy following the train of thought in their reading to be conscious of how many words per minutes they are achieving. To assure yourself that you are making dramatic progress in reading speed, you may want to use the following "speed chart" to measure your rate of reading.

How Fast Am I Reading?

No. of Words:	100	150	200	250	300	400	500	700	900
Minutes:									
1.00	100	150	200	250	300	400	500	700	900
1.25	80	120	160	200	240	320	400	560	800
1.50	67	100	134	166	200	267	330	460	667
1.75	57	84	114	143	170	228	285	400	572
2.00	50	75	100	125	150	200	250	350	500
3.00	33	—	66	—	100	133	165	232	333
4.00	25	—	50	—	75	100	125	175	250
5.00	20	—	40	—	60	80	100	140	200

a) Rule of thumb: The average page has 350 words. To get an approximate count, multiply the number of lines by the number of words per line. (You can get a rough sense of the latter by counting the words in three or four lines and taking an average.)

b) An average college graduate reads 250 words per minute (wpm). It takes him/her a few seconds more than two minutes to read a two-page article of 550 words.

c) Example: A person reading ten pages of approximately 350 words per page in ten minutes is reading at a rate of 350wpm. If the reading was completed in five minutes, the rate is 700wpm. For fractions of a minute use the table.

After a few initial measurements of this sort, you will probably find yourself gauging your speed in much larger units than minutes. You will notice that you completed a novel in less than an hour instead of taking several days of on-again, off-again reading. You will rejoice that you finished your business reading before leaving work and no longer have to cart home thick bundles of reports, proposals, and manuals for reading off the clock. Perhaps most of all, you will be gratified to see your in-box of e-mails and string of text messages and other electronic communications dispatched quickly, with excellent comprehension, rather than piling up day after day.

Above all, you will understand (and tell others) that speed-reading is not a race and not a competition. This is not a third grade experience where we slammed our pencils down or flapped our books shut as an audible way of letting class-mates know, "Ha, I finished before you did!" Instead, speed-reading is simply the process of using proven techniques to find your own comfort level with faster reading and more complete comprehension.

Therefore, no one can tell you to push on to ever-faster rates of reading. Your goal should be to master the techniques of efficient reading contained in the following chapters. Satisfy-ing progress in reading speed and comprehension will follow as surely as day follows night.

SURVIVING THE WORD BLIZZARD

You are wise, by the way, to be interested in increasing your reading speed and comprehension. Like a gradual snowfall that accumulates, foot by foot, to cover the landscape, we are all being buried a bit more each day by a word blizzard that, at least since 2000, has been dumping ever increasing quantities of words into our laps.

By some estimates, in fact, a midlevel manager in 2012 is responsible for reading at least four times the number of words per day that were required of his or her counterpart in the 1980s.

As you look around your office or home, you may not see obvious signs of this word blizzard. Yet, you probably experience its effects—the perpetual feeling that you are behind in your business reading or that you only have time to glance at documents that you know you should be reading with care. The word blizzard also strikes most of us in the form of e-mails (often more than 100 each day for many business people) and text messages, which can number literally in the thousands per month for high school and college students. Or you may experience the word blizzard as an increasing burden of "take-home" reading in your briefcase. The pile of to-do reading grows on your desk or night table, and your only hope is that documents at the bottom of the pile will become irrelevant simply by being ignored over time.

At least five phenomena account for the word blizzard now faced by virtually every professional:

◆ The explosive growth in e-mail, text messages, blogs, search-engine text, e-books, and e-zines. It is not uncommon for office workers at all levels to face thousands of words of e-mail each day. "Work," in fact, has been partially redefined in many companies as simply keeping up with one's e-mail. It goes without saying that much e-mail, even after spam filtering, is not germane to our particular business activities. We get countless messages through distribution lists that should have been sent to only a few individuals. Just as annoying, we find ourselves wading through e-mails from bosses and coworkers who like to "gab" in long, rambling e-mails. Then there is spam. In spite of filters and bulk bins, we spend valuable minutes each day getting rid of junk.

◆ What does the future hold? In spite of company policies attempting to govern e-mail use, there is no leveling off in sight for the upward trend of e-mails we receive at work and at home. Add to the thousands of words we may receive by e-mail each week the additional reading of text messages, tweets, social media prose, and many other electronic sources of reading. Even those of us who delete much of the e-mail we receive nevertheless have to spend time reading sender identifications and subject lines to determine what to send to the trash bin. E-mail intrudes steadily into our personal lives as we forward our business e-mail to home "just to keep up with anything important that comes through." Such devices as Blackberries and iPhones bring us many kinds of information in text, graphic, and auditory form on a 24/7 basis.

◆ Advances in photocopying. In the business era of our mothers and fathers, sending out a ten-page report to fifty people in the company was a major undertaking. Ten stacks of pages were set out on a long collation table. Some unlucky individual then had to walk back and forth along the line and assemble and staple the reports. The bottleneck for "papering the entire company" with our reports was distinctly physical. That bottleneck has now all but disappeared. Printing one hundred or more copies of a collated, stapled report is now no more complicated or troublesome than pressing a couple of buttons. Many more people in the company are now receiving many more pages simply because they are easier to reproduce on modern photocopy machines. (In addition to the hard-copy report, of course, we usually also receive an electronic file attachment.)

◆ Instant messaging and text messaging. You may not yet be in the habit of flashing off a quick real-time message to a coworker or friend by instant messaging (in which your message pops up on the receiver's screen) or text messaging on your cell phone, but the rising generation (let's say those under twenty-five) has embraced both of these communication technologies with a passion. An informal survey of Northern California high school students showed that students with cell phones sent and received an average of sixteen text messages per day. Those with instant-messaging capability on their computers spent an average of one hour per day in instant-messaging sessions.

There is no reason to believe that this new generation of people just entering the workforce will not carry with them the communication links they have grown up with. Imagine for a moment your own work life under siege by instant messaging and text messaging. In the midst of trying to answer your e-mail, you are bombarded by answer-me-now instant messages that flash up on your screen, iPad, or smart phone.

In the midst of responding to your voice mail, you also have to deal with a host of text messages blinking away on your cell or desk phone. (This glimpse of the future is not intended to be disparaging of new communication technologies but simply to argue that we have to prepare for them, lest we become buried in the word blizzard.)

◆ Fax and word processing. Although fax and word processing technologies are quite distinct, both add to the ease of creating and sending large numbers of texts to large audiences at the press of a few keys. In the case of word processing, text files are stored—with the inevitable possibility that they will be used again in slightly rehashed form. (Letters of reference, job descriptions, customer-response communications, and periodic reports are all especially susceptible to this use-it-again approach to texts.) The result, again, is more words headed toward your desk or electronic in-box.

◆ Books, magazines, and journals. With the advent of desktop publishing software, a renaissance has occurred in the last decade in the quantity (if not the quality) of magazines and journals. Hundreds of specialized publications have appeared, ranging from *Gift Basket Review* to *Seafood Leader* to *Dental Economics*. Not far behind in numbers of new publications are online e-zines. Books, too, have never been produced in greater quantity or variety, nor with more distribution channels (including catalogs, airport sales, online marketing such as amazon.com, and coffeehouse/bookstores such as Barnes & Noble). Books in 2012 are exponentially faster to bring to market, the time from copyedited manuscript to bound books now being just a matter of a few weeks, not months. E-books such as Kindle can evolve from manuscript to market in a matter of hours.

◆ The new television. News shows, notably CNN, Bloomberg, Fox, ABC, NBC, and CBS, have a steady "ticker" of running text along the bottom or top of the screen. Presumably we are expected to watch and listen to one story narrated by an anchorperson while at the same time reading a potpourri of other stories in abbreviated form as they march across the text portion of our television screen.

All these communication developments send a larger and larger pipeline of words, words, words straight to you. The word blizzard is a professional and personal reality for us all.

SIGNS OF EMPLOYEES WHO DON'T READ

Let's not kid ourselves. The fact that more words are headed our way each day does not mean that we buckle down and conscientiously attend to this increased word flow. Many employees, out of exhaustion with information overload, simply ignore many of their messages. Shutting your eyes and ears to the demands of the modern world is always an option, although a dangerous one in today's competitive business environment.

We all know coworkers who come to meetings blissfully unaware of the contents of a report they were supposed to read, a memo that was distributed for immediate attention, or a journal article that provided crucial background for discussion. Similarly, there are managers who let e-mail, text messages, memos, and reports pile up, with the explanation that "if it's really important they will phone me. I'm more of a telephone person."

A more general trend, however, has been noted by managers trying to get the workforce to read and respond to a simple memo or e-mail. "The problem," says one Pittsburgh executive, "is not that employees can't read. It's that they won't." A surfeit of words during the business day inevitably brings strong resistance to giving attention to any message. Information overload causes workers to "go to ground," with their hands metaphorically over their ears. A similar phenomenon has been noted by college professors, who complain not about student attendance (which is at an all-time high across campuses) but rather about the inability to get students to actually read their assignments, however short. One explanation, in fact, for increased student attendance in classes is the eagerness of students to hear the professor summarize what they, the students, should have gained from their assigned reading.

A perennial story that rings increasingly true in an era of word blizzards features a manager who sent a memo out to 100 employees. Of that number, twenty-five claimed not to have received the message. Another twenty-five said they got the message but did not read it. Still another twenty-five said they got the message, read it, but forgot what it said. The final twenty-five said they got the message, read it, and disagreed with it.

SHORTER ISN'T ALWAYS BETTER

In a somewhat desperate attempt to address the problem of nonreading employees, some companies have mandated shorter messages. The logic here is that employees will read short messages but will not read longer messages. At Ford Aerospace, for example, one vice president has championed the "half-page message—not a word more unless requested."

However, shorter messages do little to address the word blizzard if employees are simply fragmenting the message they need to communicate into a series of shorter communications instead of one cogent, albeit longer message. As one IBM manager told us, "I would rather have one complete, longer message that gives me the whole picture instead of a series of half-baked shorter messages that involve a lot of back-and-forth questions over a period of days or weeks. I spend half my week on the phone trying to clarify what these cryptic shorter messages are trying to say."

In a sophisticated business environment, it can prove difficult if not impossible to reduce complicated business matters to a headline, all for the sake of the idea that "shorter is better." Real damage to business processes can occur, in fact, in the effort to oversimplify a message just for the sake of length. As the Enron financial scandal made clear, the close details of transactions and fiduciary relationships are still vital for clear understanding by shareholders. The quick version of the situation is often a highly distorted version.

In sum, the solution to the word blizzard does not lie in smaller flakes.

A CASE OF PERSONAL AND CAREER CRISIS

Of the many managers and other workers we interviewed, one story stood out both for its poignancy and relevance. Ted R., a thirty-eight-year-old manager with a large insurance company, felt he was on the launching pad for imminent promotion to a senior management position and thereafter to vice president status in his organization. As Ted told his wife, he just had to do a bang-up job for the next year or two to assure his upward career mobility. Their large mortgage and expenses for their two young children would be much easier to handle once the promotion came through.

Ted committed himself not simply to do more than most managers but also to know more. Toward that end, he subscribed to several journals and magazines in his industry and read them cover to cover each month. He followed insurance developments in the *Wall Street Journal, Fortune, Forbes,* and *Business Week*, often using online versions. He actually read word-for-word the FYI attachments and reports that came to his desk almost daily from his bosses and other divisions in the company. He checked his e-mail and text messages on an hourly basis and responded quickly and fully to all messages. To keep up with the extraordinary flow of e-mail in his company (150 to 200 messages per day), Ted made it his habit to arrive at work by 6:30 A.M. He seldom left before 6:30 P.M. and almost always took home an armload of extra reading.

Ted noticed stress cracks beginning to appear after six months of his do-or-die commitment to his job. "I got lots of kudos at work for being on top of my projects and communicating well with my team and my boss. And others were impressed at meetings when I was able to mention some fact or statistic from a recent journal article I had read. But my home life suffered dramatically. I ate a quick dinner, usually after my family had eaten, then turned to my stack of reading and other work until midnight or so. Sunday was really the only day I tried not to work, but even on that day I usually found myself turning to a pile of business magazines and industry reports during the afternoon and evening.

"I was exhausted and it showed. I had hardly any time for my kids, both of whom were starting after-school soccer and wanted me there at the games. My wife understood why I was working so hard, but too much of the burden of parenting fell on her. We forgot what it was like to go to a movie or spend time with friends. She was getting as exhausted as I was.

"She and I finally sat down to figure out what to do. I knew I couldn't slack off on the job. The competition in my office was just too stiff. Someone else would quickly take my place if I backed off in my effort. The question came down to doing the same amount of work in less time. I didn't see how that was possible.

"I give my wife credit for putting me onto the idea of learning how to speed-read. She pointed out that at least half my day was spent processing words, either in the form of reading reports and journals or handling my e-mail and other messages. If that process could be speeded up significantly, I could actually get home in time for dinner and not have extra work to do in the evening.

"The rest of the story is pretty straightforward. I took a speed-reading course, got the hang of how to apply the skills to my business reading, and soon found myself with hours of extra time each week. I found out that I got my promotion. I think speed-reading had everything to do with saving me from a personal and professional crisis. I plan to use the reading skills I learned as I continue to climb the corporate ladder."

CONVERTING A WHIM OR CURIOSITY TO A BUSINESS NECESSITY

Ted's story helps make the point that speed-reading is among the most important skills a rising business person can master. Viewed schematically, every professional faces the dilemma of more and more information flowing toward point of meaning-making—that is, the point between the ears:

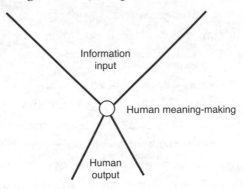

If this diagram represented a computing problem, we would resolve the dilemma by increasing the processing speed of the chip (that is, the meaning-maker). Traditionally we have been at a loss as to how to increase the processing speed in any significant way of human meaning-makers. We are not "wired" genetically for parallel processing capability—as individuals, we deal with issues and decisions sequentially, not simultaneously. Nor can we significantly increase the pace of our analysis and decision making without lessening its quality, especially when time must be provided for input and review by others. Add to these limitations the built-in constraints of many of our senses: In practical terms, we cannot train ourselves to hear more quickly any more than we can speed up our sense of smell or touch in any meaningful way.

That leaves one processing gateway that, with guidance and practice, we can rev up for increased productivity: our reading speed. To appreciate the potential power of the eyes (and the mind linked to the eyes), consider this brief mental experiment. When you take a picture of a landscape in full color with your digital camera, the file storing that picture (whether jpeg, bitmap, etc.) is many times larger than a digital black-and-white picture of a printed page. Capturing the image of the page is child's play for an eye capable of grasping and remembering the myriad complexity of a natural landscape.

In learning to speed-read, you will be drawing upon that extraordinary power of the eye to reach beyond word-by-word imaging (our first-grade lesson in reading) to larger, more complex image packages. As you learn to let your eyes and mind exert their power and range over the printed page, you will quickly grasp the secret to speed-reading: learning to see more and think more. Once you master techniques to help you extend your visual and mental range, speed itself will not be the issue. You will not find yourself "pushing" to read faster and faster, as if you were preparing a party trick of some kind. Instead, you will relax into a more complete vision of the printed page, much like a person who gradually removes blinders so that a wider field of vision becomes apparent.

PERSONAL MOTIVATION TO SUCCEED

In the same way that a first golf lesson does not lead automatically and effortlessly to success in that difficult game, so lessons in speed-reading require sustained personal motivation and practice if years of slow reading habits are to be reversed. In fact, you should put this book aside until a later time unless you are willing to commit time, energy, and patience to the adventure of speed-reading.

Simply knowing what to do to read quickly is comparable to knowing what to do to run faster. Knowledge alone will not increase your reading speed or your running time. As with any skill, knowledge must be accompanied by application, practice, and repetition. After all, you are asking your eyes and mind to view the printed page quite differently from the way they are used to perceiving it. At this point you have already spent thousands of hours using "slow habits" to read. Now you must commit a very small fraction of those hours to reprogram the eyes and mind for a new way of seeing, comprehending, and remembering. In literal physical terms, your brain needs a bit of time to develop new neuropathways to make possible new ways of seeing and understanding the printed page.

To provide that time of growth and make your commitment to speed-reading specific, use the following Mastery Plan as a "contract with yourself" to set personal targets. Writing down your scheduled goals will help to assure that speed-reading becomes more than a nice idea in your personal and professional life.

Time commitment

◆ Four hours (recommended) to read this book and work through its exercises. Target completion date: _____.

◆ Thirty minutes per day for three weeks in applied reading (of your choice) to train the eyes in new reading habits. Target time each day: _____.

CONSIDERING COMPANYWIDE APPLICATIONS

As you experience the advantages of speed-reading for your professional life, you will no doubt consider the beneficial changes that such a program could bring to particular groups or the entire workforce within your company. Appendix A presents sample syllabi that can be used by your training department (or training specialist in a smaller company) to deliver a speed-reading program in a series of half-day sessions.

Companies and organizations that have put on speed-reading training programs for their employees include IBM, NASA, Citibank, Lockheed Martin, Apple Computer, New York Life Insurance, Xerox, the White House, Verizon, United Airlines, American Stores, Ford Motor Company, and many others. Typical feedback from such programs is highly positive:

From a financial supervisor: "Through speed-reading I opened up at least two hours each day on my schedule."

From a line manager: "I spend less than a third of the time than I used to devote to reading reports, bulletins, and product information. I'm reading more in less time."

From a senior manager: "I used to hate wading through personnel documents and endless federal and state advisory memos and letters. Using speed-reading, I get this work done in a fraction of the time it used to take. I haven't had to take work-related reading material home for months."

GREAT EXPECTATIONS

The greatest motivator for success in any skills-based program, including speed-reading, is your conviction that good things—very good things—will happen as a result of your expenditure of time and energy. Among the benefits you can reasonably expect from this program in speed-reading are the following:

◆ More free time to explore creative and innovative opportunities inside and outside your company.

◆ More thorough comprehension and retention of business materials you read.

◆ A wider range of business reading, as your increased speed allows you to extend the type and scope of reading that interests you or impacts your job.

◆ Less intrusion of business reading into your personal life. Speed-reading can allow you to experience an eight-hour work day again, perhaps for the first time in years.

◆ Less nausea at the thought of reading business reports, proposals, and other documents, many of them poorly written. You will have the confidence that you can whip through such reading in record time while simultaneously increasing your comprehension and retention.

◆ Greater career success as your ability to acquire and retain knowledge increases dramatically.

SUMMING UP

Speed-reading is not a trick. It is a proven way of seeing more on the page or screen—and thinking more about what you see—through efficient use of eye movements and focus. For many professionals increasingly buried under more and more words, speed-reading offers the last, best hope for completing work while at the office rather than extending the business day by bringing home sheaves of late-night reading or saved electronic files.

Free Reading

Although this chapter has not focused on specific techniques to speed your reading, you can nonetheless begin your exploration of the topic itself by looking online at some of the Internet sites devoted to speed-reading. You can find these sites, along with recommended books and videotapes, in the Resources section at the end of the book.

Chapter 2

Understanding Why We Read Slowly—and How to Change

◆

"Every moment of one's existence is growing into more or retreating into less."
—*Norman Mailer (1923–2007)*

THIS CHAPTER ANSWERS FOUR QUESTIONS:

◆ What can I expect at the beginning of the learning curve for speed-reading?

◆ What is subvocalizing, and how does it affect my reading speed?

◆ What causes backtracking?

◆ How can the problem of porous concentration be solved?

The last two decades have witnessed the dramatic rise in professional coaches for rising managers and executives. These coaches help their clients to recognize which habits are working well for them in business and which are holding them back. For example, coaches may work with managers and executives on such matters as making presentations, hosting company visitors, conducting meetings, and evaluating the performance of subordinates. Some coaches even teach rising executives which wines to select at dinner meetings and how to "work the room" at social occasions.

"It's amazing," one coach confided to us, "that the bright individuals I work with often can't see the most obvious things they are doing wrong. They remind me of someone with his finger stuck in a door—but who just continues to press on the door. People like this have become so used to doing business in habitual ways that they have great difficulty switching over to better ways, no matter how logical and apparent they may be. They won't let themselves just open the door and take out their finger."

ESCAPING DECADES OF BAD READING HABITS

Being stuck with slow reading habits is like having your finger stuck in a door. The clear, simple message of this book is "you can take your finger out of the door." If you are reading more slowly than you would like, you probably are falling back on flawed reading behaviors you have used for many years. Those habits feel like "you" and other approaches no doubt feel strange at first.

Step one, then, in setting aside bad reading habits is the realization that change (of any kind) is not going to feel familiar, cozy, and reassuring at first. Trying new reading behaviors will feel awkward for a time, in the same way that your first attempt to strum a guitar or keep your skis parallel probably felt somewhat unnatural. Some learners make the mistake of interpreting these signals of strangeness and difficulty as a sign that "this just isn't for me. I can't do this." It's a good thing that pilots don't turn their planes around to land at the first sign of turbulence.

You, too, will have to steel yourself to a few minor bumps at the beginning of the learning curve on your way to reading more quickly. Techniques and behaviors that feel strange for the first half hour of practice will feel much less so during the second half hour and may begin to feel comfortable shortly thereafter. Do not quit at the first feelings of awkwardness.

Step two is more general in nature but no less important: Be patient with yourself, as you would be with anyone else trying to overcome decades of habitual behavior. Praise yourself for your progress and, for that matter, for simply making the effort to jump out of the rut of inefficient reading approaches. You are committing yourself to dramatic improvement in reading, one of life's most crucial professional and personal skills.

FIVE PITFALLS THAT SLOW READING TO A SNAIL'S PACE

Precisely what has gone wrong in the past with our reading proficiency, in spite of years of education? Here's a hit list of five mini-disasters that have befallen us, beginning with our earliest school years:

1. **Subvocalizing.** Readers in the grip of this unfortunate habit have the problem of "hearing" every word they read. What their eyes see on the page becomes "sounded out" in the mind (not literally with the voice). The experience is not unlike an echo chamber, where the visually perceived words on the page echo as sounds (as if someone were reading aloud) inside the reader's head.

   Subvocalizing slows reading down by paying too much attention to words one by one instead of in combination, as "meaning packages." We do not let our mind move on until we hear the words somewhere in our head. This habit often springs from our earliest days as readers in kindergarten or first grade. There we were proud to be able to read each word on the page aloud to our teacher and classmates. Despite the decades now separating us from Ms. Fisher and first grade, many of us continue to "read aloud" within our minds.

Bear in mind that we speak (or read aloud) at a rate of 175 to 225 words per minute, while we are capable physically and mentally of reading visually (without the subvocalizing component) many times faster than that rate—and with an increase in comprehension to boot. The key lies in learning to see packages of words rather than in hearing individual words in our mind. Subvocalizing makes it impossible to treat words in "chunks" rather than one by one.

2. **Backtracking.** This reading pitfall predisposes readers to regress phrase by phrase through the paragraph or page. After seeing and grasping the content of one phrase (perhaps three to six words in length), the reader's eye habitually leaps back to the same phrase or a previous phrase

before moving on to new material. This "one step for-ward, two steps back" approach to reading makes the completion of even a single page the work of several min-utes instead of a few seconds. Studies have demonstrated that college graduates tend to backtrack about twenty times per page.

Readers who backtrack in this way often do so in response to an inner "guilt" voice (perhaps from a parent or teacher) that keeps saying, "Are you sure you have understood? Are you sure you haven't forgotten anything? What did you just read? What came just before that?" These voices have to be turned off and ignored for reading speed and comprehension to improve. The new "script," or inner voice, replacing the "guilt script" says something like this: "Of course I understand and I'm reading ahead quickly to increase that understanding." In other words, we all have to have confidence that achieving meaning lies a step ahead of us in our reading—in the next paragraph, on the next page, and so forth—rather than behind us in phrases and sentences we have already read. In this way, we can view ourselves as explorers continually pressing forward toward discovery rather than nervously looking back over our shoulder every few seconds to see where we have been.

3. **Porous concentration.** Some readers are obsessed with the self-criticism: "My mind is a sieve. I read a few sentences and almost immediately forget what I've read." Except in the extremely rare cases of short-term memory loss (made immortal in the 2004 movie *Fifty First Dates*, with Drew Barrymore and Adam Sandler), forgetting "everything" we

have just read is an expression of our worries, not a reality. As you will experience even in your first lessons on speed-reading, you do retain and can discuss remarkable amounts of what you read. Furthermore, you can put the pieces of your reading together with your own thinking to come up with original perspectives that the writer did not conceive of or anticipate. In other words, you have the ability not only to think with the writer but also to step ahead of the writer to draw your own implications and conclusions.

If you fear porous concentration, or the "sieve" effect, you are probably making one of two common mistakes. First, you may be trying to "parallel process" as you read— that is, have your eyes on the page while your mind is attending to several other priorities. Concentration will be porous indeed if you are thinking ahead to a special date, making mental menu choices for lunch, and tallying your VISA bill all while you are supposedly reading a page. Simply focusing on the task and pleasure of reading will avoid the pitfall of porous concentration.

Second, readers experiencing porous concentration may be the adult victims of childhood pestering, in which a teacher or parent kept insisting, "Tell me what you just read. Can you repeat the information point for point?" Reading is not preparation for rote repetition or photographic memory of the page. Bugging ourselves, even subconsciously, to be capable of such repetition or instant recall is a sure formula for diffusing the very concentration we were trying to achieve. Speed-reading—and any effective reading, for that matter—involves relaxing our way into the flow of meaning as it delivers itself to us from the page. One superb speed-reader likens the act of efficient reading to drinking a glass of cold water: "You simply drink it in at a pace that's comfortable for you, without worrying unduly about the process of swallowing. If you think too much about the process either of swallowing or reading, you'll choke!"

4. **One-gear reading.** Your mountain bike or car adjusts its gears to the task at hand, whether climbing a steep road or whizzing downhill. Yet, snail-paced readers are "stuck in first gear"—that is, they have not made adjustments in their reading speed according to the difficulty or importance of the reading material at hand. If we are considering whether to take a new medication for an illness or injury of some kind, we may well read slowly and carefully through the fine-print page of pharmaceutical information and contraindications that accompany the prescription. However, that microscopic, life-or-death reading speed is certainly inappropriate for a Stephen King novel.

You may have shaken your head in disbelief, in fact, as your significant other plows through several books on the night table while you mark your pages again and again over the course of a week or more to get through a single novel. Clearly, your partner is revving up his or her reading speed by choosing a "gear" appropriate to the material at hand. You, on the other hand, may be staring at Stephen King sentences with the same slow earnestness that you might rightly use when reading the Declaration of Independence. That's how books become overdue at the library!

5. **Your attitude toward new learning.** Finally, you may be at a comfortable plateau of life where no one is pushing you to new mental achievements. No one is forcing you to work more quickly, finish a novel in an evening instead of a week, or complete your work at the office instead of bringing it home. If you inhabit such a pressure-free space in life, how fortunate for you—and what an ideal time to take up a new, exciting, and rewarding skill like speed-reading. When was the last time you took a long leap of faith toward a new area of learning? Some of us have to go back to college days (or even back to our first attempts to ride a bicycle) to remember what it was like to take a learning risk, to master some new skill set or body of information.

If you are phobic about new learning ("I might fail! It might be harder than I thought!"), your attitude will undercut your motivation and eventual success. Better to approach the new learning involved in speed-reading as an adventure that promises to bring you unexpected benefits and enjoyment, as it has for millions of others. Such optimism about the learning process will keep you eager to understand the progressive steps toward speed-reading mastery in this book and to undertake the important practice exercises with diligence and focus.

SUMMING UP

Most of us come to speed-reading lessons as average readers held back in our reading efficiency by the combined forces of subvocalization, backtracking, porous concentration, one-gear reading, and unhelpful attitudes toward new learning. Speed-reading take us step-by-step up a gradual but quickly mastered learning curve that results in truly remarkable improvements in reading speed and associated comprehension and retention.

Free Reading

Reach again for a favorite piece of light, entertaining reading—perhaps a novel you have wanted to read or a best-selling nonfiction book. Read ten pages or more with an eye open to your own habits. Specifically, try to observe whether you subvocalize, backtrack, experience porous concentration, engage in one-gear reading, or hold on to unproductive attitudes toward new learning. You may want to keep notes on your own specific reading barriers so that you can watch them recede and eventually disappear under the influence of new reading strategies and skills.

Chapter 3

Learn to Jog, Not Walk, Through Your Reading

◆

"To know the road ahead, ask those coming back."

—Chinese proverb

THIS CHAPTER ANSWERS THREE QUESTIONS:

◆ What is underlining, and how can it speed my reading?

◆ What is a pacer, and how is it used?

◆ What is soft focus, and how does it make use of my peripheral vision?

If you have ever been to a dog-racing track, you know that the greyhounds sprint around the track not to beat one another to the finish line but instead to catch that pesky mechanical bunny that sprints ahead of them—always just a hare's distance, so to speak, in advance of their noses.

This chapter will introduce you to the mechanical rabbit, as it were, that will get you jogging (and soon running and sprinting) instead of walking through your reading. You will need three items for this lesson:

◆ A pen you can hold comfortably in your hand for sustained periods of time.

◆ A prose book of low-to-medium difficulty with lines of print that run all the way across the page (in other words, in one column, not two or three). A novel typically will suit just fine. Do not use this speed-reading book (this page, for example) as your sample reading material. You will be reading this instructional material in a different reading "gear" than we want you to use for your initial experience of underlining.

◆ The courage to try something new in your reading habits, even if this new technique reminds you of a very early stage in your reading education.

LEARNING TO "UNDERLINE"

We have placed the word *underline* in quotes (at least in its initial occurrence) because we do not want you to make ink marks under any of the words in your book. Instead, you will learn to let the motion of your pen flow about a half inch above the paper, as if you were quickly underlining or high lighting the lines of print. Your pen will move along beneath the line you are reading so as not to obscure your vision of any of the words. (You recall this motion of the hand from high school or college, when we all underlined or highlighted practically every passage in our assigned reading prior to a test. Perhaps you remember pages highlighted from top to bottom in yellow—our reassurance that we had "really studied" for the upcoming test.)

Strive for a flowing rhythm of your pen, left to right across the page and just below the sentences, down the paragraphs, to the bottom of the page. Don't rush and don't dawdle. Try to maintain an even, comfortable pace. Take a moment right now to try this motion. Don't worry for now if your eyes are not tracking precisely with the movement of your pen or if you do not feel you are "reading" the words rushing by. The goal for right now is simply to get the mechanical rabbit, as it were, running smoothly on the track. We'll worry about catching it in a few minutes.

Why a pen instead of your finger? There is no hard and fast rule here, and many highly proficient speed-readers do use their pointer finger instead of a pen as their pacer. For those just starting out, however, a pen has at least three advantages over a finger:

◆ The point of the pen provides a somewhat sharper point of focus than does your finger. When we get to the triple-chunking technique, that sharper point may be more helpful than a broad fingertip.

◆ The practice of running your finger beneath words may remind you of your first elementary school experiences in reading and to that extent may be the wrong mindset for learning new skills.

◆ The finger—including the shape or condition of the nail, the color of the nail polish, and so forth—can be a distraction to some readers. Especially if the reading at hand becomes a bit boring, one's finger may be more interesting by comparison!

Time Out

Take a few minutes to practice the underlining motion. Perform this motion on the following passage until underlining feels smooth and natural. Let your eyes follow along as the pen moves across the page, but do not be discouraged if your eyes backtrack at times. Keep your pen moving at an even, reasonable pace.

Todd Mallek, 40, sells heavy industrial equipment for a major industrial broker on the West Coast. He is married without children and travels two weeks a month on average. "My job is pretty much like Las Vegas. You spin the wheel and hope for a major score. If it doesn't come, you spin again. As long as it takes. When I started out in this position six years ago, I got discouraged too easily. I remember one time in particular. I flew all the way up to Seattle from L.A. to meet a prospective customer. The guy had me spend most of the day with him going around to different job sites and looking at various pieces of equipment he already owned. It was typical Seattle weather—cold rain—and I came back with the flu. And all for nothing. He bought from my competitor the next day for the same price I was offering him. I just about quit that day. But then there are the good days, when orders and commissions come in one on top of another. Those are the days that keep me going. Now my philosophy is this: get out there and put in the legwork meeting new customers and understanding their operations. Eight contacts out of ten may lead nowhere, but if the remaining two buy equipment, it's fat city on payday. Traveling around as I do, I hear about job opportunities with other companies. But the reason I stay here is the upside potential. What else could I be doing that would net me six figures in a good year? I tell the new salespeople that there's only one trick to having a really good year: avoid the post-honeymoon syndrome. This is when you wine and dine a new customer to the point of his or her first purchase or two, then gradually lose interest as you pursue new customers. Customers should never be considered 'in the bag,' as I tell our sales force, and you shouldn't treat them as if they were. Since I'm the senior person now and usually hit the top numbers each year, the company is having me do some of the sales training for the new guys. It cuts into my own calls a bit, but I enjoy talking about something I know so well. And, although the company doesn't know it, I'm going to hit them up one of these days for a bonus based on the gross sales of the people I train."

FOLLOWING THE MOVING PEN AS YOUR PACER

Now that you have practiced the natural, flowing movement of the pen, let your eyes start to pay attention to the language flowing by. Do not fixate on word-by-word reading, but instead let your eyes glide across the sentence as your pacer moves beneath it. The flowing rhythm of movement will quickly become a pattern for your brain and will replace the start-stop or regression patterns that previously slowed the reading process. Your first experience at following your pacer may not be entirely successful. Relax. You are unlearning eye movements practiced for decades. No wonder it will take a bit of practice to let your eyes flow freely with your pen/pacer instead of stopping to look at the letters of particular words or to "subvocalize" these words in your head.

As you practice, try to avoid consciousness of one word at a time. Instead, let your peripheral vision see "chunks" of prose (three or four words to a "chunk," or package). Seeing multiple words at a time makes it easier for your eyes to keep up with your moving pacer.

REPLACING YOUR PEN OR OTHER PACER FOR ON-SCREEN READING

It is obviously not practical, and often destructive of the screen, to run a pen or other physical pacer across the plastic or glass of your electronic device (smart phone, iPad, computer screen, Kindle or other e-book screen, and so forth). Touching the screen with your finger as a pacer can also be problematic, since many screens are touch-sensitive and will respond to the press of your finger in a variety of ways you don't want.

Therefore, many successful speed-readers have perfected a simple trick for reading on electronic screens. They hold a finger just a bit above the screen without touching it. Importantly, your finger should be placed somewhat *below* the portion of text you are reading. You want to make sure that your eyes have every opportunity to scan, even at a subconscious level, "what's coming" in the ongoing flow of prose. When we perceive even in minimal ways a clue or two about what's ahead in our reading, we're able to better comprehend and retain the text portion being read.

You will be reminded in the instructions for on-screen exercises in this book to use your finger as a non-touch pacer. With practice, of course, your eyes will begin to read down the screen without need of a pacer.

STARTING TO SEE THE BIG PICTURE THROUGH SOFT FOCUS

Speed-reading strategies all emphasize the important connection between the words within a sentence and the surrounding words (and ideas) in the paragraph, page, and larger units of organization. By moving relatively quickly through this context, you are more likely to glimpse the big picture (or major, organizing ideas) of the prose at hand. Imagine, by comparison, looking at an oil painting one inch at a time, from top to bottom, without being able to see beyond that square inch. Details of the painting would be confusing to you because they occur out of context. As the saying goes, you would be likely to miss seeing the forest because of all the trees.

The smooth-scan underlining process you are learning requires a "soft focus" of the eyes rather than the hard focus you may be more familiar with. Hard focus occurs when we stop to examine a word at a time, as if examining individual butterflies pinned in a collection. Hard focus "bores in" on a narrow frame of view, while soft focus relaxes the boundaries of vision and tries to perceive what's on the right and left as well as what is in the middle of one's view (the middle being marked by the point of your pen/pacer).

Time Out

Take a moment right now to read ten or more pages of relatively light and entertaining reading using your pacer and striving for relaxed soft focus that grabs chunks of words rather than focusing on individual words. (Again, use the material described at the beginning of this chapter for your reading. Don't try to pace yourself at this point through pages within this book or anything formatted in double or triple columns, such as a business magazine or a newspaper.) Again, a reminder: if you are reading on-screen, use your finger as a pacer slightly raised from the screen.

FINE-TUNING THE PROCESS

In reading your ten pages or so in the Time Out exercise, were you conscious of your head moving slightly from side to side in response to the back and forth rhythmic movement of your pacer? If so, steady your head. You should not appear to be watching a tennis game while reading. In fact, only three "systems" should be involved at this point in the underlining stage of speed-reading:

◆ The moving pen, which establishes a pace for reading.

◆ The eyes, which, through soft focus, see chunks of words instead of individual words.

◆ The mind, which assembles the ever-increasing ideas and images aroused by the words into meaningful patterns and messages (the "big picture").

Studies of speed-reading programs reveal that up to one-third of all speed-reading participants settle upon the underlining technique alone and rely on it to speed up their reading significantly, as it certainly can. In other words, their learning curve peaks out with the underlining technique. However, we titled this chapter "Learn to Jog, Not Walk, Through Your Reading" to suggest that there are "gears," or reading speeds, easily accessible to you through other techniques beyond underlining. Later chapters will show you how to run and sprint in your reading to reach truly remarkable levels of reading speed and comprehension.

For now, congratulate yourself on breaking free from one-word-at-a-time hard-focus reading. You can reap the benefits of improved reading speed through underlining if you practice, practice, practice. Your brain, after all, is involved in the amazing process of establishing new neuropatterns to replace patterns of eye movement and focus rehearsed over decades of your life. The new learning (underlining) you are now trying to make habitual comes as an invasion of sorts to the status quo of the brain. As the conscious mind (what you *want* to do) struggles against the inertia of the brain (with its established patterns for what you usually have done), a "war" of sorts is taking place. Learning can be viewed as your mind winning the war of innovation against long-established brain patterns.

SUMMING UP

Using a pen as a pacer will stimulate your eyes to "flow" across the printed line rather than attend to individual words.

Soft focus that uses your peripheral vision will help you become aware of packages, or "chunks," of words rather than individual words. Checking your comprehension using the practice exercises will reassure you that you are understanding and remembering what you are reading. Although some speed-readers stop their instruction at the underlining stage, we urge you to continue on to several techniques described in the following chapters to maximize your reading and comprehension levels.

PRACTICE SESSION 1

Directions: Use your pen to pace the movement of your eyes through the following test selection passage. Then take the comprehension quiz to gauge in a general way your success in understanding what you have read. If you do well on the quiz, move on to the next practice session. If you do not do well, repeat the reading exercise to make sure you can locate the correct answer. After you have read all passages and have taken the comprehension quizzes, reread the passages more quickly by moving your pen at a faster back-and-forth rhythm and making a conscious (but relaxed) effort to practice soft-focus perception of "chunks" of words, not individual letters or words.

Note that we are not calculating words per minute of reading speed at this point. Too mathematical a focus on your initial progress fights against the strategies of achieving a natural, relaxed pace and comfortable soft focus.

TEST SELECTION
Chunking and Crunching Is So Easy

Question: Is chunking a practical skill or just a theory?

Answer: You use chunking every day when you break a telephone number into its segments of area code, prefix, and last four digits (415-555-2929). Our short-term memory is more comfortable with small packages of data rather than one long string.

Question: How does chunking apply to speed-reading?

Answer: In speed-reading, we mentally divide long strings of words (such as the words running across each line of this page) into a maximum of three sections or phrases. Traditional reading habits for educated people, including college graduates, have focused on a word-by-word approach. In a twelve-word sentence, for example, traditional readers stop to focus on and mentally hear each word (not counting minor connectors such as *and* and *but*).

Question: Does it really matter whether I read in chunks or word by word?

Answer: Would you rather walk from Los Angeles to San Francisco or drive your car? Chunking is simply a more efficient way of getting where you want to go in your reading. You can reduce the time it takes to read an article by two-thirds. Put another way, you can read three articles in the time that traditional readers take to read one article. Furthermore, you will comprehend more and remember what you read more completely. In professional or academic settings, speed-reading gives you a competitive edge. The skill of chunking can be mastered with only ten minutes of practice each day for a period of about three weeks.

Question: What proof exists that chunking speeds the reading process?

Answer: Harvard Professor George A. Miller published a still-famous article in 1956 titled "The Magic Number Seven Plus or Minus Two: Some Limits on Our Capacity for Processing Information." Miller's work established the principle that chunking improves the reader's comprehension and ability to remember. He demonstrates that readers understand and remember more if the writer offers an average of seven points (not less than five and not more than nine). Going beyond the "chunking limit" of seven points is an almost inevitable recipe for losing the attention of your readers.

Question: Do we experience information overload when we try to process too many discrete items of information?

Answer: Exactly. Speed-reading packages these individual items into segments that allow the reader to see a minimum of three words simultaneously. Snail-paced readers, on the other hand, mentally say each word to themselves and, as a consequence, lose their concentration an average of twenty times per page. These gaps in concentration prove disastrous to understanding and memory. Instead of grasping the content of what we are reading, our minds flit away to unrelated thoughts—our next vacation, an upcoming date, or a sports event.

Question: I understand chunking, but what is crunching?

Answer: Crunching is combining and condensing words on the page. In effect, you learn to "see" strings of words as if they had no spaces between them. By practicing the crunching technique, you unlearn and resist the third-grade habits of subvocalizing—that is, sounding out syllables in words, as if a voice inside were reading words to you one at a time and very slowly.

Question: Can I speed up the rate at which I perceive words simply by using my willpower?

Answer: In the same way that an untrained, poorly conditioned runner cannot will himself or herself to break track records, you cannot simply say, "Today I will read twice as fast as I did yesterday." Learning techniques for speed-reading (in other words, training and conditioning) empowers you to read more quickly. However, once you have learned those techniques, you can exercise your willpower to push your achievement level ever higher. You can use the phrase "Speed up!" at the beginning of each paragraph as a mental prod to leave traditional reading habits behind and soar to new speed and comprehension levels.

Questions for Practice Session 1

1. How does a telephone number demonstrate chunking?

2. What idea did Harvard Professor George A. Miller demonstrate?

3. Using chunking, how much faster (on average) will you read?

4. Approximately how often do traditional readers lose their concentration per page?

5. What is crunching?

6. What is subvocalizing?

7. What phrase can speed-readers use at the beginnings of paragraphs to increase reading speed?

Answers for Practice Session 1

1. A telephone number is divided into segments.

2. Miller showed that people comprehend best when points are limited to an average of seven.

3. Three times faster.

4. Twenty times per page.

5. Perceiving groups of words simultaneously as if they had no spaces between them.

6. Mentally saying syllables or individual words as you read.

7. "Speed up!"

PRACTICE SESSION 2

Follow the same general directions for the reading selection and comprehension quiz in this session. However, this time, challenge yourself to move your pen/pacer more quickly across the page—perhaps increase your speed 25 percent or so over the pace you used in Practice Session 1. Next take the comprehension quiz for the reading. As in Practice Session 1, go back to reread the passage after you have successfully passed the comprehension quiz. If your correct answers on the comprehension quiz show that you are understanding what you read, continue to push ahead the pace of your pen (without making reading a frantic or unduly stressful experience). If you answer incorrectly on the comprehension quiz, repeat the reading exercise and maintain your present pace for the time being.

TEST SELECTION
Eye-Blinking

Did you know that your degree of attention changes the rate of your eye-blinks? When you mechanically move your eyes across a sentence—left, middle, and right—your attention shifts once, twice, three times. When you read one word at a time, you do not control your attention—it is random and s-l-o-w.

Who cares?

If you are blinking your eyes rapidly—more than 30 times per minute—you are wandering mentally and have lost your concentration. Further, the faster your eyes blink beyond the norm—15–30 blinks per minute—the greater your anxiety and stress.

When you are stressed by an interview, exam, presentation, or relationship, you negatively affect your long-term memory, concentration, and comprehension, and you reduce your reading and learning skills by up to 40 percent. Test scores go down.

What can you do about it?

When you squeeze your facial muscles, scrunching your eyes, mouth, and cheeks, you release the tension in these muscles.

Squeeze and hold for five seconds, one-one-thousand, two-one-thousand... We have six muscles in each eye, four rectus and two oblique, and when we choose to exercise them by squeezing, electrochemical reactions release our stress, and we return to normal blinking. Use this strategy at the appropriate stress and panic moments. Do it for one minute and relax, and you will function at your maximum.

Anything else?

When you exercise your eyes by choosing to look upward toward your eyebrows and downward to your lips, and then left and right, you trigger the twelve eye muscles. This exercise awakens your lazy peripheral vision, created by the rods in your retina. The photoreceptors—rods and cones—transfer information electrically through fibers to your brain.

A greater use of our peripheral vision produces the ability to speed-read chunks of sentences instead of merely one word at a time.

The entire exercise requires one minute of your time, and should become a habit before a learning session, as well as to relax your eye muscles before stressful events.

Here's how it works scientifically speaking.

Emotion from our limbic system stimulates the RAS (Reticular Activating System), triggering the midbrain, which releases dopamine. Dopamine controls our rate of blinking.

We automatically blink faster when face-to-face in a romantic encounter, when speaking to a group, during anxiety and stress, and when lying. Under stress we blink 75 percent faster than normal—that is the time to use your one minute exercises. You might want to remember that prior to lying there is an eyelash flutter.

Questions for Practice Session 2

1. What is the "title" of this article?

2. When we read one word at a time, which mental skill becomes random and slow?

3. True or false: normal eyes blink approximately 60 times per minute?

4. How many muscles do we have in each eye?

5. Name one strategy to release your "stress" before a test?

6. What exercise awakens your lazy peripheral vision?

7. How much time does the exercise in question 6 take?

8. When people lie, speak in front of a group, or are in a romantic situation, do they blink faster, slower, or normally?

9. True or false: dopamine alone controls the rate of blinking?

Answers for Practice Session 2

1. The title is "Eye-Blinking."

2. Reading one word at a time, your attention becomes random and slow.

3. False: a normal eye blinks 15–30 times per minute.

4. We have six muscles in each eye.

5. Squeeze your facial muscles, and scrunch your eyes, mouth, and cheeks.

6. Looking upward, downward, left, and right.

7. 60 seconds.

8. Faster.

9. True.

PRACTICE SESSION 3

The following exercise imitates the kind of reading we all do on-screen for e-mails, text messages, tweets, and so forth. Use your finger as a pacer, raising it slightly above the paper as if you were avoiding the touching of a screen. After reading the e-messages in the exercise, take the comprehension quiz and then check your answers. If you find that you missed more than 20 percent or so of the questions, re-read the passages without slowing down (since you have already read the material once).

Imagine that you receive the following text messages within a ten minute period. See how quickly you can read them and how much you recall from what you have read.

TEST SELECTION
Grasping Text Messages Quickly

Hi. We're free for dinner tonight and are wondering what you guys are doing. Do you want to try some new restaurant or would you rather do a barbecue over at our house? It looks like the weather is going to be nice—no rain for a change.

(one minute later)

Just talked with my wife and she isn't getting home from work until 6:30 or so. Probably the restaurant idea would work better for us. What about you? What kind of food? We haven't had Chinese for a long time, but that maybe isn't your first choice. Just let us know and we'll try to make some reservations.

(one minute later)

Idea: We could have Chinese food delivered over here, since my wife probably won't feel much like cooking after getting home late, and maybe watch a TV movie or something. You don't need to bring anything—or maybe just a bottle of wine, if you want. I don't know why, but I like white wine with Chinese food. But go with whatever you like and have on hand. Let's say 7:15, OK? Let me know if any of this works for you. We can also go out if the take-out food idea doesn't appeal to you.

Questions for Practice Session 3

1. Why was the time 7:15 suggested as the arrival time for dinner guests?

2. Has the decision to order "take-out" Chinese food been finalized?

3. What other types of ethnic foods are named in these messages?

4. What are the guests supposed to bring with them to the meal?

5. Other than eating together, what other activity might the dinner group engage in?

6. What preference for food is expressed by the wife of the person writing these messages?

7. Is a barbecue at the message sender's home still an option?

8. Who is supposed to pick up the Chinese food?

Answers for Practice Session 3

1. The message sender's wife will not be home from work until 6:30.

2. No. The invited dinner guests can still indicate that they don't want to order take-out Chinese food.

3. No other ethnic foods are named.

4. White wine.

5. Watching a TV movie.

6. The wife expresses no preference.

7. No. The message sender says that his wife won't feel like cooking after arriving home late from work.

8. No arrangement has been made for who will pick up the Chinese food or pay for it.

Free Reading

Turn to something you like to read—a favorite novel, perhaps, or a nonfiction book on a subject that interests you. Use the underlining technique to make progress in speed-reading through practice. As much as possible, let your pacer move almost automatically without being particularly aware of it. Similarly, let your eyes fall with soft focus on chunks of words. If you find yourself falling back into the pattern of word-by-word reading or subvocalization (saying words "aloud" in your mind as you read), don't be overly concerned or self-punishing. Simply recognize that new behaviors take time, especially when ingrained habits must be replaced. When you catch yourself in an old habit, just switch back to techniques such as underlining and soft focus that will guarantee increased reading speed.

Chapter 4

Learn to Run, Not Jog, Through Your Reading

◆

"Slight not what's near, while aiming at what's far."

—*Euripides (ca. 484–406 B.C.E.)*

THIS CHAPTER ANSWERS FOUR QUESTIONS:

◆ What is indentation, and how does it alter the underlining process?

◆ What is soft focus, and how can it be used to see more at a glance?

◆ What are the advantages of using peripheral vision to see to the left and right of as well as above and below the point of soft focus?

◆ How can I use the beginning and ending letters of words to speed perception?

Your next steps in the speed-reading process will help you consolidate your gains from underlining taught in Chapter 3. They will also build upon those skills to add 50 percent or more to your reading speed.

INDENTING

The first step or skill we will work on in this chapter is called "indenting." Although justified margins in letters, memos, and books have made paragraph indentation less common these days, we all still recognize the familiar inset of five letter spaces or so when it occurs at the beginning of a paragraph. The original purpose of such indentation was to let us know that a new paragraph was beginning. (A blank line serves the same purpose in documents using justified margins.)

For our purposes, however, indentation has a special meaning. It refers to a more sophisticated and efficient way to underline. Using the technique of indenting, your pen will no longer move under the entire line. Instead, it will begin about two words in (estimate, don't count) from the left margin and conclude its movement about two words in from the right margin. Your eyes, as always, should follow the pen. Don't let your eyes drift to a hard focus on the first word at the beginning of the line while your pen is already moving a couple of inches into the line. Similarly, don't let your eyes settle into a hard focus on the last word of the line while your pen has already moved to its indented position at the beginning of the next line. Train your eyes to stick with your pacer even if an occasional word or two escapes you. Remember that you are always reading for "big picture" comprehension. Hard focus, as familiar as it may feel and as tempting as it may be, is not your friend in achieving reading speed and improved comprehension.

Use your pen/pacer to follow along the indented line as you read the following material. Let your peripheral vision pick up the first few words and last few words in each line. To help your eyes, track with your pacer using the indented pathway. Repeat this reading exercise several times.

One important goal for Todd Mallek is making the sale. His physiological needs (food, shelter, clothing), economic security, social relations, sense of esteem, and other factors all depend in part on closing the deal. To achieve this end, Todd is willing to engage in a period of goal-directed activity. Note that this activity (which can include business travel, product presentations, phone calls, and so forth) does not in itself fulfill Todd's needs listed above. In fact, if he were only to engage in goal-directed activities without ever achieving the goal itself (the sale), he would be looked upon as a failure by his company and colleagues—a well-intentioned, hard-working but unsuccessful salesperson. Early in his career Todd perceived the relation of goal-directed activity to goal fulfillment as a small investment for a big payoff. In this period of his life, he couldn't bear to put too much legwork into a sale; he had to see "results" (goal fulfillment) to keep his confidence and energy up. With experience, however, Todd became more content with a different model. He became more willing to put in a large investment of effort in hopes of even a relatively modest payoff. In other words, he gained confidence in his eventual success and therefore was willing to undergo long periods of goal-directed activity without actual goal fulfillment. Todd's hard-won sense of patience and confidence can be attributed in part to his powers of visualization and memory. Todd carries within himself powerful and stimulating memories about past sales. He remembers holding large commission checks in his hand. He recalls the loud applause when he was recognized as Salesperson of the Year by his company. He sees the sales achievement plaques decorating his office wall. In all these ways, Todd participates in imaginative goal fulfillment even while in the midst of his goal-directed efforts. Todd Mallek's motivation, in sum, is based largely on his expectations. His efforts on the job intensify to the extent that he believes goal-fulfillment to be likely. If he concludes that goal-fulfillment is unlikely no matter what he does, he probably will withdraw his effort completely.

Why Indent?

You can probably guess the purpose of this revised form of underlining. Your hand now has less to do (cutting down its total movement by 20 percent or so) while your eyes are forced to perceive the "edge" words in a line of prose through peripheral vision. In effect, your eyes are being trained to move farther away from the old word-by-word reading routine and toward the perception of chunks of words. Because many electronic screens such as those on smart phones are small, you should shrink your zone of eye focus to a relatively narrow band centered down the middle of the screen. Use your finger, raised slightly from the screen, to help train your eyes to concentrate comfortably on the middle zone while also being as aware as possible of words to the left and right of the middle zone.

Time Out

In a self-chosen piece of relatively easy reading, practice the indentation technique for at least ten pages. If you find it difficult to "grab" the first couple of words in your peripheral vision, slow down your pacer a bit. Do not compromise its placement in the indented position of each line. Realize through this practice that you really can see and take note of the beginning and ending words of a line without specifically looking at them; they are there in your conscious understanding of the line of prose, but you have not had to spend mental or physical effort actually focusing on those words. Just as your pacing hand now has much less to do, so your eyes have had a burden of 20 percent or so lifted from them in terms of the work they (and the brain) are expected to do in the act of reading. One important key to speed-reading lies in finding easier ways for the eyes, mind, and brain to do their cooperative work. Speed-reading teaches our perceptions to work smarter, not harder.

Reflecting on the Indentation Process

Snail readers (which include most of us from traditional educational backgrounds) have become used to a visual perception span of six to eight consecutive letters at a time. In other words, these readers can focus on a word series such as "on a trip" (seven letters) in one perceptual focusing act, but they must focus and refocus several times to perceive, let's say, thirty consecutive letters, as in the phrase "on a trip to Portland to visit an aunt."

Although the idea of seeing such a large group of words in one focal act may now seem beyond you, have faith and "stick with the program." Accomplished speed-readers go beyond the narrow focus of their foveal (retinal) perception span to capture in one view thirty-five letters or more in their peripheral vision. Imagine the reading speeds possible if you were able to focus once on six or more words at a time instead of one word at a time. Nor need we focus on the superstars of speed-reading to make the point. Even average speed-readers in their first few lessons quickly master the technique of expanding a single focus to include three or four words. That ability alone *triples* reading speed, and because more words are seen in mutual context, comprehension rises 15 percent, as does long-term memory retention of what's been read.

Try this visual experiment. Direct your soft focus to the OOO pattern that appears in the middle of the page. As you do so, try to be aware of the number patterns on either side of the OOO. Practice this experiment several times; with each repetition try to gather more information from your peripheral vision about outlying patterns of numbers without actually redirecting your focus to those patterns.

301 OOO 251

692 301 OOO 251 892

916 692 301 OOO 251 892 916

438 916 692 301 OOO 251 892 916 792

Now try the same exercise with words instead of numbers. Notice that words are easier to grasp in peripheral vision than are number strings. Also notice that words that have a context of some kind (a sustained pattern of meaning) are easier to perceive in peripheral vision than are unrelated words. Remember to direct your soft focus only to the OOO portion of each line. Remember also that you are learning to expand your peripheral vision. Don't conclude, "I just can't do it," if you reach an initial limitation of one or two words on either side of the OOO focus point. With practice you will be able to see more and more words in one soft-focus perception.

Rich OOO handsome

elevated rich OOO handsome green

tuna elevated rich OOO handsome green although

caught a large tuna yesterday OOO using only a minnow for bait

SPIN-OFF ADVANTAGES OF PERIPHERAL VISION

As we have seen, your ability to "see" to the sides of your direct focus allows you to pick up extra words without focusing specifically on them. Your improved peripheral vision allows you not only to "reach" to the beginning and end of a prose line but also to scan or visually explore a bit to the words above and below the prose line. Even before you began your study of speed-reading, you probably experimented with this "above-below" view when you were just trying to get the gist of, let's say, a long descriptive paragraph in an exciting novel. You were eager to get on to dialogue and action and so "scanned" the long descriptive paragraph just to grab a few main words and impressions.

Now you can include that behavior as a valuable part of your speed-reading skill set. By opening your perceptions to what lies just above and below the line you are reading, you gain significant insight into the author's context. Observing surrounding words in this way gives you "heuristic ability"—that is, the ability to predict in advance where ideas are leading and to understand them more completely thanks to that "early warning system." Like a basketball player getting ready to intercept a pass or block a shot, you prepare your moves on the basis of what you see coming at you. In peripheral reading, you are able to think more completely about what's being said because you perceive more pieces of the word puzzle at one time.

Time Out

Take a moment to read at least ten pages of some light reading (using your pen/pacer, of course, and the indentation technique), but this time with your eyes and mind open to the possibility of spotting (but not focusing on) key words above and below the line you are reading. In some cases, these words may be several lines away from the specific line you are looking at. Let your mind play freely with the additional images or ideas these "extra words" introduce to your thinking and feeling.

To begin this practice process, direct your soft focus only to the OOO pattern in the following example. Let your peripheral vision be aware not only of words to the right and left of the OOO, but also of words in the lines above and below the OOO.

6 percent of Americans

actually own a flag OOO and put it on display

during national holidays OOO and civic celebrations

FREEING YOURSELF FROM DEPENDENCE ON THE WHOLE WORD

How much of a word do you need to see before grasping its meaning and moving on with the sentence? The answer to that question varies by context, but in general we require only the beginning two or three letters of a word and perhaps a letter or two at the end to make sense out of the word. Test this principle by looking at the following series of "words," which progressively have more and more of their middle letters missing:

```
noth    g
bec    se
expl   n
swim    g
matt   s
deo      nt
tele     n
```

You can speed your reading dramatically by not looking at each and every letter within a word.

When we see words in context, we require even fewer letters to make out their meaning. In the following sentences the same words that appear on the previous page have been shortened even more, but you will still be able to quickly guess their meaning with a high degree of accuracy:

I looked inside the bag but there was no   g there.

She broke up with Frank b   se he insisted on living with his parents.

The detective could not exp   n how the burglar got into the house.

We went to the beach for an afternoon of sw   g.

The movers delivered the bed frame and mat   s.

We decided just to stay home and watch tel   n.

The medicine cabinet contained only a stick of deo   t.

You do not have to decide which letters to ignore. That mental busyness would end up slowing down your reading. Simply get over the notion that you have to "see everything" on the page in order to be a good reader. As demonstrated here, you will find that you can read with excellent comprehension and remarkable speed by actually "seeing" only 20 to 30 percent of the printed marks on a given page. You are skipping over nonessential marks and focusing on the marks that contribute most to meaning.

Time Out

With the thought in mind of letting your eyes fly along with your pacer without seeing every mark on the page, choose about ten pages of light and entertaining reading for this reading exercise. Use the pacing and indentation techniques you have learned along with soft-focus and peripheral vision. In this exercise, also try to put into practice the principles of focusing on the top of the letters, not the middle or bottom, and on the letters that matter most to meaning (usually the first few letters and a last letter or two).

SUMMING UP

Indentation shortens the "sweep" of your pacer and requires your eyes to glimpse, in peripheral vision, the beginning and end of lines. Peripheral vision, with practice, enables you to see word "chunks" to the left and right of and above and below the focus point. Your eyes do not need to see entire letters to make sense out of words. The first few letters and the last letter or two almost always reveal the intended word, particularly if that word is used in a context.

PRACTICE SESSION 4

Directions: Use your pen to pace the movement of your eyes through the following passage. Then take the comprehension quiz to gauge in a general way your success in understanding what you have read. If you do well on the quiz, move on to the next practice session. If you do not do well, repeat the reading exercise to make sure you can locate the correct answers. After you have read both reading selections and have taken the comprehension quizzes, reread the passages more quickly by moving your pen at a faster back-and-forth rhythm and making a conscious (but relaxed) effort to practice soft-focus perception of "chunks" of words, not individual letters or words.

TEST SELECTION
Foods That Heal

We know about the good foods, the fruits and vegetables, the grains and greens that are supposed to fill our plates. And we try to eat them. But often it's the same old apple, steamed broccoli, and salad, meal after meal, that makes eating right a chore; it also means that you're denying yourself some remarkable treats. There are delectable foods that just happen to be potent medicine.

Asparagus: a good low-calorie source of folate and potassium, and stalks that are high in antioxidants. Prized as a springtime delicacy for centuries, this edible member of the lily family is now so widely cultivated that it is available in every season.

Asparagus provides essential nutrients: six spears containing 135 mcg (micrograms) of folate, a third of the adult RDA (recommended dietary allowance), 545 mcg of beta carotene, and 200 mg of potassium. Research suggests folate is the key in taming homocysteine, a substance implicated in heart disease. Folate is also critical for pregnant mothers, because it protects against neural tube defects in babies. Asparagus is low in calories (just twenty in six spears), yet it gives you fiber and important antioxidants such as glutathione.

Chilies: an excellent source of beta carotene and vitamin C. They may help to relieve nasal congestion, and help prevent blood clots that can lead to a heart attack or stroke.

A popular ingredient in Southwestern cooking, chilies—or hot peppers—add spice and interest to many foods; some of the milder varieties are consumed as low-calorie snacks.

Chilies are more nutritious than sweet peppers, and the green ones have a higher nutritional content than the red ones. They are a very good source of antioxidants, especially beta carotene and vitamin C. Just one raw, red hot pepper contains about 65 mg of vitamin C, nearly 100 percent of the RDA. Chilies also contain bioflavonoids, plant pigments that scientists believe help to prevent cancer. Capsaicin, the ingredient that makes chilies hot, may act as an anticoagulant, perhaps helping to prevent blood clots that can lead to a heart attack or stroke. Medicines use capsaicin to alleviate the pain of arthritis and shingles and mouth pain associated with chemotherapy. These capsaicinoids, when transferred to the face, can cause severe eye irritation.

Grapefruits: pink and red varieties contain both beta carotene and lycopene, potent antioxidants. High in vitamin C and potassium, low in calories, they contain bioflavonoids and other plant chemicals that protect against cancer and heart disease. Grapefruits are especially high in pectin, a soluble fiber that helps to reduce blood cholesterol. Lycopene, an antioxidant contained in grapefruit, appears to lower the risk of prostate cancer. A Harvard study involving 48,000 doctors links ten servings of lycopene-rich food a week with a 50 percent reduction in the rate of prostate cancer.

Kiwifruits: an excellent source of vitamin C and a good source of potassium and fiber. They can be used as a meat tenderizer. They taste tart with overtones of berries. They originated in China, but were adopted by New Zealand farmers, who named them for the national bird. They are now a major crop in California and are kept in cold storage for year-round consumption. They contain pectin, a soluble fiber that helps to control blood cholesterol levels. Kiwis also contain lutein and zeaxanthin, antioxidants associated with eye health.

We end by suggesting that you also add mushrooms, which boost immune function, to your regular diet. Last, we suggest you consume sweet potatoes. They taste great, are an excellent source of beta carotene and antioxidants, help reduce cholesterol, and may prevent diverticulosis.

Questions for Practice Session 4

1. How many foods are discussed in detail?

2. What's so great about asparagus?

3. Which of the leading diseases does asparagus help you avoid?

4. What part of the U.S. loves to cook with chilies?

5. What leading disease do chilies seem to prevent?

6. What two leading diseases does grapefruit protect against?

7. Where did kiwifruits originate?

8. What two other healthy foods are recommended as an afterthought?

Answers for Practice Session 4

1. Four.

2. High in antioxidants, low in calories, and helps pregnant mothers. (Any of these three benefits is correct.)

3. Heart disease.

4. Southwest.

5. Cancer.

6. Heart disease and cancer.

7. China.

8. Mushrooms and sweet potatoes.

PRACTICE SESSION 5

Directions: Use your pen to pace the movement of your eyes through the following passage. Then take the comprehension quiz to gauge in a general way your success in understanding what you have read. If you do well on the quiz, move on to the next chapter. If you do not do well, repeat the reading exercise to make sure you can locate the correct answers. After you have read both reading selections and have taken the comprehension quizzes, reread the passages more quickly by moving your pen at a faster back-and-forth rhythm and making a conscious (but relaxed) effort to practice soft-focus perception of "chunks" of words, not individual letters or words.

TEST SELECTION
Seniors Arise!

Beginning at around age forty, there are three signs of aging that apply to vision, and as we age, they significantly affect the quality of life.

One: The lens of the eye becomes rigid and fragile, while the six muscles in each eye, which focus the lens, become atrophied and degenerate. The result in middle age and later in life is the inability to focus on small print.

Two: The cornea begins to yellow, and there is considerable difficulty perceiving colors. In fact, 65 percent of those affected cannot see shades and gradations of colors. Color is the domain of the cones in the retina—7.5 million of them—while seeing in dim light (night vision) is mediated by the rods—125 million of them. Both cones and rods—our photoreceptors—lose their elasticity and become dormant or permanently inactive with age.

Three: The retina withers, and with less light able to enter the eye, visual acuity—sharpness of focus—deteriorates, and one's surroundings appear murky. The fovea centralis (the area of most accurate vision), located in the macula lutea (of the retina), also degenerates. Reading becomes downright difficult—even with glasses, which usually tend to have thick lenses.

Are glasses the exclusive solution?

Typically, the strength of our eyeglass prescriptions increases annually. There are simple medical procedures now that can be done in the office with local anesthesia using laser surgery. In the first decade of the twenty-first century, the lens, the cornea, and the retina can be regenerated to offer almost 20/20 vision—which is often not the case with glasses.

How significant is the loss of shading in vision?

Inability to read newspapers, paperback books, even text on the Internet is a serious blow to cognition. Research indicates that Alzheimer's and dementia are held at bay by the mental exercise of learning and the acquisition of information. Those seniors who do not engage in the use of their mental faculties on a daily basis have twice the incidence of Alzheimer's and dementia. Specifically, reading nonfiction that requires the use of organization, logic, reasoning, and long-term memory creates a "firewall" against debilitating brain diseases. Playing card games, such as bridge, that require continuous decision making exercises synaptic firing and thus help maintain the integrity of the axons and dendrites of our neurons. Underutilized neurocircuits atrophy and are in time extinguished. The cliché "Use it or lose it" is apt when referring to brain cells.

Labels

Informed consumers read drug labels for survival. A recent study recorded that 91 percent read the front label on the box, while 42 percent read the label on the back of the box. The reason for this disparity was that the size of fonts was usually much smaller on the back label. When drug executives were queried, their response was that designers, mostly in their mid-twenties, were unaware of the challenges of seniors.

Colors

Finally, aging also causes visual difficulties when the background on which printed text appears provides too little contrast. In an advertising research project, 75 percent of those over forty years of age have a major challenge in differentiating between the colors green and blue. Both appear as a shade of yellow. The solution is the use of black, white, and red.

Questions for Practice Session 5

1. What group does the article target as readers—seniors, advertisers, or drug companies?

2. How many major signs of vision-aging did the author discuss? *3*

3. Name those you recall. *cornea, lens, retina* ~~color, labels, reading games~~

4. What percentage of the aging population cannot perceive shades of colors? ~~94%~~ *65%*

5. There are two types of photoreceptors that manage vision. What are they? ~~retina~~ *Cones and rods*

6. What do you recall about the fovea centralis? *area of most accurate vision*

7. What new procedure is used to improve vision? *laser*

8. The incidence of what two degenerative diseases is reduced by cognitive activity? *Alz + dementia*

Answers for Practice Session 5

1. Seniors.

2. Three.

3. Lens, cornea, and retina.

4. 65 percent.

5. Cones and rods.

6. It is the sharpest area of visual acuity; it is located in the macula lutea of the retina; it is used especially in reading.

7. Laser surgery.

8. Alzheimer's and dementia.

PRACTICE SESSION 6

Imagine that you receive the following string of e-mails within a five minute period. Use the eye movement techniques described in this chapter to grasp the content of the e-mail string as quickly as comfort allows. Push yourself a bit, since we all tend to settle into a pace for e-mail reading that may be somewhat slower than we use for, let's say, reading a novel.

TEST SELECTION

To: Brenda Johnson

From: Fred Williams, Manager

Subject: Planning Vacation Time

Hi, Brenda. Thanks for your request for vacation during the first week of July. Have you figured out which of those days come from your regular vacation days and which are public holidays? I would say "yes" right now to your request but, as you know, we follow a seniority system in coordinating vacation times. Linda and Juan still have to check in with me to let me know what their requests are. I'll be back in touch soon and, in the meantime, if you have any questions, just call me—it's easier than e-mail for me.

To: Fred Williams, Manager

From: Juan Ortiz

Subject: My vacation days

Fred, I have some flexibility at the beginning of July for vacation, but I do have to be gone (for a wedding) on July 6, no matter what. Will this work for you? I haven't checked with Linda yet. I know she has seniority over me, but I'm hoping that something like a wedding will be given special consideration no matter what the usual policies are about vacations and seniority. Thanks for getting back to me right away, since I need to buy airplane tickets to get to the wedding.

To: Fred Williams, Manager

From: Linda Brown

Subject: Vacation seniority

Hello, Fred. If I have calculated correctly, I think my seniority gives me first choice of vacation days. Therefore, I would like to take off from June 26 through July 6. I haven't let Juan and Brenda know, because I don't feel it is my place to figure out how they are going to work out their vacation dates. But in any case, you know now what days I'll be taking. Thank you.

Questions for Practice Session 6

1. What is the last name of the office manager?

2. What has Fred decided about which employee will have first priority to take vacation during the first week in July?

3. What was the first name of the employee who wanted to attend a wedding?

4. What reasons did Brenda give for wanting to take the first week in July as her vacation period?

5. Does the company count public holidays as vacation days subtracted from the total vacation period given to employees?

6. Why did Linda contact Brenda and Juan before writing an e-mail to Fred?

7. What e-mail communication has passed between Juan and Brenda before Fred receives Brenda's e-mail?

8. Which employee ranks higher in the seniority system—Juan or Brenda?

Answers for Practice Session 6

1. Williams.

2. Fred has not decided.

3. Juan.

4. Brenda gave no reasons.

5. No.

6. Linda did not contact Juan and Brenda before e-mailing Fred.

7. No e-mail communication has passed between Juan and Brenda.

8. Juan.

Free Reading
Apply the techniques learned to date (underlining, indentation, soft focus, and using the beginnings of words) for a relaxed reading experience of at least thirty minutes on reading material of your choice.

Chapter 5

Learn to Sprint, Not Run, Through Your Reading

◆

"What you do speaks so loudly I cannot hear what you say."

—*Ralph Waldo Emerson*
(1803–1882)

THIS CHAPTER ANSWERS SIX QUESTIONS:

◆ What is triple chunking, and how does it influence the movement of my eyes and pacer?

◆ How can the words "left, middle, right" help me retrain my eyes for most efficient soft-focus points?

◆ What is "target affirmation," and how can it keep me from bogging down as I speed-read?

◆ How can I achieve double and single chunking to speed my reading?

◆ What is the Z pattern of eye movement, and how does it maximize my use of peripheral vision?

◆ What is the reverse-S pattern of eye movement, and how does it offer an alternative to the Z pattern?

To this point, you have practiced four techniques that, used together, have undoubtedly increased your reading speed significantly:

◆ underlining with your pacer

◆ indenting to view the beginning and end of a line in your peripheral vision

◆ using soft focus to see "chunks" of words instead of individual words and to glimpse key words above and below the line you are reading

◆ seeing just enough of a word to grasp its meaning

The lessons in this chapter will continue to use all these techniques while adding on new "warp speed" skills that will allow you to read even faster while also maximizing comprehension.

TRIPLE CHUNKING

How many parts does a single line of prose have? Most people would simply count the number of words in the line and give that number as their answer. Speed-readers, however, become used to dividing each line into a left, middle, and right focus point, or "target." With practice, the brain creates a new neuropathway for this triple-chunking approach to the printed line (replacing the word-by-word pathway ingrained from earliest elementary school years).

Notice that the same chunking technique comes to the rescue when you are trying to remember telephone numbers, social security numbers, and other extended strings of digits. You can appreciate the power of chunking by viewing the following numbers in their "unchunked" and "chunked" forms:

Telephone number: 9175552938   (or)   917-555-2938

Social security number: 321549876   (or)   321-54-9876

That same principle applies to series of letters and words. Using soft focus, we grasp chunks of information more easily and more memorably than by viewing the same information in its discrete parts.

Retraining the eyes and mind to "triple chunk" each line of print instead of following word-by-word requires a bit of patience, a sustained period of practice, and a new way of thinking about "reading." For the purposes of this chapter, you will have to postpone your eagerness to achieve high levels of comprehension (these will be restored soon). Training the eyes and mind to triple chunk necessitates a period of practice where all that matters is the left-middle-right, left-middle-right, left-middle-right rhythm of focus on each line. It doesn't matter for now what the line means. You could literally turn your reading matter upside down and practice this left/middle/right exercise just as successfully.

Note that your pacer continues to flow in the same way as before, but now it makes very brief pauses at the left, middle, and right portions of the printed line. Your eyes (and mind) continue to follow the lead of the pacer in stopping at three soft-focus points for successful triple chunking.

Use your pen/pacer to follow along the line. This time, let your pacer move smoothly to three intermediate positions (soft-focus points) within each line, as indicated by the line. Try to grasp all the words in the line in three soft-focus "stops." Peripheral vision will help you see a chunk of words instead of a single word or two. To help train your eyes in the rhythm and pattern of triple chunking, repeat this reading exercise several times.

Some readers find it handy at first to mentally recite the words left, middle, right as they retrain their eyes and brain to triple chunk a printed line. Try this technique. If it works, continue to practice it until your way of viewing a line becomes so habitual that you no longer require a prompt. If, on the other hand, you find the phrase is disturbing your focus and concentration on triple chunking, abandon it. Our mutual goal is to find what works for you.

Victor Vroom has helped a generation of managers understand the inner workings of expectancy motivation. Vroom points out that expectancy involves three key factors:

If you believe that your effort affects your performance

(and)

If you believe that your performance determines predictable outcomes

(and)

If you believe that you value those outcomes

(then)

You will be motivated to expend maximum of near-maximum effort.

In Todd's case, he first expects that his personal investment of energy (in the form of sales visits, travel, phone calls, and so forth) will affect his performance as a salesperson. "No one has success handed to him," Todd likes to say. Second, he expects that his performance will lead to predictable outcomes. His contract with the company, for instance, specifies that he will be paid a certain commission rate per sale. Finally, Todd knows that he values both the financial rewards and the prestige of being a top salesperson. But remove any one of Vroom's three components and motivation evaporates. Let's say, for example, that Todd felt his sales were a matter of luck, not effort. Or imagine that the company simply wouldn't pay him his earned commission. In either case, Todd's motivation to work would virtually disappear. Finally, imagine that Todd (perhaps because of some spiritual conversion) decides to resist the allure of money. If work outcomes lose their meaning to him, motivation to achieve work results ceases entirely.

On average, the technique of triple chunking, once mastered, adds 60 percent to one's reading speed and 15 percent to comprehension. That's an attractive reward for the time and energy you will spend teaching your eyes and mind to "see" a printed line in a new way.

Time Out

Reach for your chosen piece of light and entertaining reading. Read at least ten pages using the triple-chunking approach. Don't be discouraged if your eyes at first want to make several "focus stops" on the line. Simply forge on, striving for left-middle-right chunks of perception. If you feel your comprehension has slipped a bit in the process, don't worry: the goal for now is instilling the triple-chunking technique as an automatic way of seeing and thinking.

TARGET AFFIRMATION

Any sustained, repetitive activity can become wearisome after a while. As you work your way through an extended piece of reading, you may inevitably feel your reading speed start to slip and old word-by-word habits creep in again.

To prevent this problem, use the technique of "target affirmation" to renew your overall sense of purpose and your specific goals. Here's how the technique works: At the beginning of each paragraph, silently (but forcefully) say to yourself, "Speed up!" That command alone, as simple as it sounds, will keep the mechanics of your speed-reading skills—underlining, indenting, triple chunking, and so forth—working smoothly and even gaining speed as you move through a document.

We observe the use of target affirmation every day in all aspects of life. The basketball coach shouts "Block the shot!" from the sidelines as a stimulus and instruction to a defensive player. A collection letter concludes with "Pay your bill within forty-eight hours or service will be terminated"—and gets much better results from debtors than a letter ending with "your account is overdue." A parent tells a child, "Finish your chores before you go out to play," and a CEO tells his or her employees to "beat the competition" in the marketplace.

All such commands are potent in their power to move us from a state of thinking to a state of action. Although external commands can "get us off the dime," the most powerful commands are those we give to ourselves—the commands, in other words, to which we give the highest priority. Among such internal commands are personal prompts such as "You can do this!" "Save your calories for later!" and "Don't overreact, no matter what the other person says." These are target affirmations in the sense that we set a behavior target—something we want to achieve—and then urge ourselves on (or "affirm" our effort) to reach our goal.

Obviously in speed-reading, the most helpful target affirmation is "Speed up!" That phrase, spoken silently but passionately at the beginning of each paragraph, prods us to apply new principles and techniques that do not follow the status quo of our reading habits from elementary school on. We need a frequent internal reminder to press on with skills that may feel somewhat strange but which day by day begin to prove their worth by converting us from snail-paced readers to cheetahs.

Time Out

Using your chosen item of light and entertaining reading, read ten pages while practicing the "Speed up!" target affirmation at the beginning of each paragraph. Make sure you say this command to yourself with assurance and urgency. If you don't mean the command, you probably won't heed it.

ADVANCED STRATEGIES FOR SUPER-SPEED-READING

Three special add-on skills will predictably lift your reading speed another 75 to 100 percent and perhaps more. There's no reason to put off experimentation and practice with these skills until you have become something of an expert with earlier techniques taught in this book. Some speed-readers will take to these advanced techniques right away—so much so that they may wonder why they took the time to learn the earlier basic skills. For most of us, however, the following strategies fit best in our speed-reading program after we have developed confidence and capability in the underlying components of speed-reading.

DOUBLE CHUNKING AND SINGLE CHUNKING

If a line can be successfully divided into three chunks for purposes of quick perception, why not two or even one? As mentioned earlier, our powers of peripheral vision make it possible to perceive as many as thirty-five words in a single chunk or cluster. We can literally "see" an entire line of print in two soft-focus stops, or even one, along the line, using our ever-present pacer.

Time Out

Try to double chunk the following prose lines by making a soft-focus stop approximately at the dot beneath each half of the line. As a stimulus to keep your eyes moving onward, use your pacer to move to these dots. Don't make lasting judgments about your abilities to double chunk on the basis of this one exercise. Read it several times to get the "feel" of the double-chunking rhythm and technique. Then choose ten pages of light and entertaining reading for practice on your own in double chunking.

Use your pen/pacer to follow along the line, this time with two soft-focus stops (double chunking). You will have to rely even more on your peripheral vision to grasp a larger chunk of words at each focus stop. To help you train your eyes in the rhythm and pattern of double chunking, repeat this reading exercise several times.

Todd's dilemma is precisely the motivational sinkhole into which many urban employees find themselves. Their ostensible rewards—a salary, let's say of $60,000 per year—ceases to have meaning when housing costs skyrocket, child care expenses soar, and crime rises. The reward aspect of the green paper symbols received in the pay envelope begins to pale; the dollars buy less and less satisfaction. Employees in less commercially intense regions of the country or the world have learned to capitalize on this reality for motivational purposes. "Come to Kansas," one employment ad reads, "where a good salary still buys a great life." As economic imbalances increase between regions, many employees find themselves trapped beneath an area's reward ceiling. A talented agricultural chemist in Montana can't afford to accept his company's offer of a transfer to the home office in New York. His two acres and spacious home in Montana couldn't be re-created in New York for several times his salary, if at all. One final aspect of expectancy motivation involves the availability of necessary environment factors. Let's say that I believe that my effort to sell freezers to Eskimos will affect my sales performance; I believe, further, that my company will indeed pay me for every freezer sold; and, finally, I believe that I value those dollars. However, if the subzero environment makes freezers unnecessary, my motivational supports (in other words, my reasons for trying) fall like a house of cards. Entrepreneurs often face this motivational waterloo. Without adequate market studies, they assemble a ground-floor staff and set off with great enthusiasm to franchise the world or achieve some other sales goal. When the enterprise fails to achieve results, the boss too often (and incorrectly) examines only the three motivational components. Why aren't my employees giving their best? Do I have to increase salaries or commissions? Do they want something besides money? The culprit in this lack of motivation may be availability. The region or economy may be to blame, not the motivational level or sincerity of the employees. A CEO's dollars, in other words, should sometimes be spent on market research and development rather than employee pep talks and other perks.

Of course, a single focal stop along each line would speed the process even more and allow your pacer to move vertically down the page (with one soft-focus stop in the approximate middle of each line) instead of sweeping back and forth.

You may surprise yourself by how much of a line you can actually see in peripheral vision with a relaxed soft focus at the center of the line. Ironically, your power to "see" an entire line will increase as you worry less about accounting for each and every word, as you did in the old snail-paced reading mode. Try to achieve a "seeing-Europe-from-the-train-window" frame of mind. Your goal is to experience the countryside rushing by your view, not to count cows or name particular trees or flowers. As you ease into this more relaxed approach to comprehension, you will discover that your mind gathers up many more impressions and much more data than you consciously intend.

Time Out

Use the dot beneath each of the following lines as your single soft focal point in experimenting with single chunking. Again, do not be discouraged or make lasting negative judgments if your initial experiments in single chunking are frustrating. There is no rule that says you must double or single chunk to prove your worth as a speed-reader. Of the many techniques available, you will eventually settle upon the set of skills that feels most comfortable to you. There is no "black belt" award among speed-readers for any particular level of chunking.

Use your pen/pacer to follow along the line to its single soft-focus stop at the approximate middle of each line. Stretch your powers of peripheral vision to glimpse as much of the line to the right and left as possible. To help your eyes learn the admittedly challenging pattern of single chunking, repeat this reading exercise several times.

Peggy Woodward, thirty-five, is one of six midlevel managers in the San Francisco office of a commercial credit firm. She is single and has sole caregiving responsibility for her elderly mother.

Am I getting what I deserve at this company? Yes and no. Yes, for my education level and experience, I'm getting a better-than-average salary for this industry. The benefits package is good, and we have a profit-sharing plan that adds a few thousand dollars to my retirement plan each year. But no, I'm not getting what I deserve when it comes to this specific office and some of the things that have been happening here. Last month, for example, all six of us in the midlevel management range found out about our raises: 5 percent for each of us across the board. I went home stunned that day. Any objective observer of the company would have seen that, over the past year, four of us have been working like dogs and the other two—I'll call them Alice and Ruth—have been absolutely loafing. Last year my immediate boss gave us all a sermon about merit raises—how we would individually be rewarded for our effort. Like fools, four of us took that message seriously. We came in early, left late, often skipped lunches, and even spent some Saturdays on the job. Alice and Ruth, however, found every excuse in the book to be away from their desks. They each took their maximum number of sick days, got permission to attend off-site management seminars, and generally treated their jobs as a hobby. On several occasions, Ruth's subordinates had to come to me for information and decisions that she was responsible for.

Z IS FOR ZORRO

Some speed-readers find that, as they see more key words in peripheral vision above and below the line they are reading, they don't have to devote soft-focus points to each and every line. They can sweep past some lines because they have already grasped the content of that line from their peripheral view.

This is the so-called Z pattern of reading. Picture three lines of prose, each labeled by a number for our purposes. Begin the Z technique by using your pacer, as usual, to move (after indentation) from left to middle to right across line 1 (assuming, in this example, triple or double chunking). Next, instead of repeating the same pattern on line 2, sweep from right to left across that line to reach the beginning of line 3, which is read following the same pattern used to read line 1.

Repeat the Z pattern as you move down the page. Note that you are not making a soft-focus stop on the line in the middle of the Z pattern. Your eyes sweep past it (but are nonetheless taking in information from it) as you move to the bottom line of the Z pattern for focused reading.

Time Out

Practice the Z pattern of reading by using either triple- or double-chunk focus points on the top and bottom lines of the Z, as shown in the example, and sweeping over the intermediate line (the diagonal portion of the Z). As cautioned earlier, don't become discouraged by your initial experimentation with this technique. If it doesn't feel natural to you right away, this approach may be a strategy you return to later as you play with your speed-reading options.

Use your pen/pacer to follow along the Z pattern of the line as you use chunking (triple, double, or single) to read one line, then sweep diagonally across the next line (viewing it peripherally) to reach the beginning of the third line, which you will again read in your chosen style of chunking. To help train your eyes in the Z pattern, repeat this reading exercise several times.

Consider Peggy Woodward's point of view. She has no complaint about her salary or benefits per se; in fact, she admits they are better than average for the industry. Nor does she dislike her work tasks in themselves. What bedevils her, however, is the mismatch between her effort/reward ratio and the effort/reward ratios of some of her peers in the company. She is losing motivation, in other words, because of what she perceives as a lack of equity. This problem of perceived inequity plagues many organizations in their hiring and compensation decisions. Let's say a business school, for example, hired new Ph.D. instructors in the 1990s for $80,000 per year. The salaries of these men and women have risen year by year, according to the school pay schedule, so that by 2005 they were earning $115,000 on average. When the school goes out to hire new Ph.D. instructors in 2005, it finds that owing to market conditions these candidates cannot be attracted to teach for less than $150,000. The result is both obvious and interesting. The school will not alter the pay scale of the employees it hired in the 1990s just because it has to pay a new instructor $150,000. Yet these older instructors, who have labored for the school for years, feel cheated because they are working for less money than the "new kid on the block," who so far has contributed nothing to the school. This mismatch in salary between the low-salaried old-timers and the newcomer is a guaranteed formula for equity disputes and motivational crises in the workforce, particularly among those who have been with the school for many years.

BIG-Z SPEED-READING

In the course of these chapters, the envelope of peripheral vision has widened from three words at a time (in triple chunking) to six or eight words (in double chunking) to a dozen or more words (in single chunking), with extra words above and below the line thrown in for good measure, thanks to the powers of peripheral vision. You will now expand that same concept to include two or more entire lines perceived primarily through peripheral vision as you sweep down the page in a vertically elongated Z pattern.

Specifically, you will be reading the top line of the Z left to right according to your chosen pattern of chunking. Then you will make a broad diagonal swath (two lines or even more) on your way to the right-side beginning of the line representing the bottom of the Z, which you will read using the same pattern you used for the top of the Z. This broad-sweep Z pattern then repeats as you move down the page.

Challenging? You bet! Again, there is no right or wrong, better or worse, about this technique over any other. It does, of course, offer the promise of speeding up your reading (perhaps by another 20 to 40 percent) when practiced effectively, but you must be the judge of whether the technique fits your comfort level, especially with an eye toward your comprehension needs. You may find that the big-Z approach works well for you with some kinds of reading (a periodic report at work, for example, that contains a great deal of pro forma, boilerplate prose). No matter what you conclude about the big-Z approach from your initial experimentation, don't banish it from your radar screen of possibilities. You may decide to come back to this technique for serious practice and mastery at some later date.

Time Out

In the following examples, use your pacer to follow the approximate big-Z line shown. The first example places two lines in the diagonal sweep of the Z. The second example places three lines in the diagonal, and the third example places four lines there. A key to success with this technique is opening and relaxing the mind. Don't press yourself to memorize anything or worry about what you will or won't recall. Simply read with speed and interest. Say your target affirmation—"Speed up!"—before beginning each example.

Once you have experimented with the big-Z pattern in these three examples, read each a second or third time to get the feel of how this extension of the Z pattern can make the most of your peripheral vision. Surely your experimentation here will demonstrate how much you really do "see" beyond the line you are ostensibly looking at.

Richard Young, twenty-five, is a systems analyst for a Miami computer company. In that capacity, he accompanies sales-people on their calls and offers technical advice on what hardware and software they should buy for particular applications. Richard is engaged to be married within a year.

I have very strong opinions about my present job. Not that anyone in the company is listening. I expect to quit soon. If it weren't for the expenses of my upcoming marriage, I would probably be out the door already. Here's what I face. This company is making money hand over fist, even in a slow economy. Everyone wants to upgrade their old computers to the new models. Making sales is like shooting fish in a barrel. I walk into a client's company with a salesperson who usually knows next to nothing about computers but is personable and attractive. He or she introduces me as a computer expert. The client describes the problem, and I come up with the computer solution.

Usually it's a true no-brainer. If the client needs more processing power, we sell a better CPU. If the client needs more terminals, we sell a network to link his or her PCs. I could do the job in my sleep. But getting back to my point, the company is getting rich on these easy sales. And what happens to those profits? In its infinite wisdom, the company's executive committee has decided to spend heavily on a "stimulating work environment" for employees. So in my office I have a $4,000 walnut desk, three leather chairs, and some original, signed artwork on the wall. We have an expensive new "dining lounge" instead of the old coffee room. We're driving Lincolns as company cars instead of Chevrolets, and of course, we each must have a new cell phone every year. Thanks to the executive committee, I'm now the proud owner of a benefits plan that will pay for anything, anytime, anywhere. Don't get me wrong. These fringe advantages are nice, and friends nearly keel over when they walk into my luxurious office. But what do all these trappings have to do with my job?

What do I think about my job? I'll tell you the truth. I think the company is underutilizing me. I'm paraded around like some kind of swami to offer a bit of techobabble to sell a client on a few PCs. The company should be going after more challenging sales. I would love to get involved in more complicated computer solutions for business or government. I'd like to go after big fish and get rewarded accordingly if I brought them in. The company thinks it's making me happy by giving me thick carpets and more flextime. But the truth is that not even more money will keep me from looking elsewhere for work. I don't mind working hard when I'm using and building my skills. But I don't like treading water, even in the executive Jacuzzi.

THE REVERSE S

If you rounded the corners of the Z pattern, you would have a Reverse S. This slight alteration makes a big difference for some speed-readers, who find not only that the S is a smoother, more flowing pattern for the pacer as the reader moves down the page but also that the S can expand or contract according to the density or difficulty of the material being read. In other words, the S pattern takes away any rigidity about how many lines (one, two, three, or more) fall within the portion earlier described as the diagonal line of Z. The S pattern simply meanders down the page as if it were a river, taking a relatively broad course through easy terrain and moving into tighter loops in more difficult territory.

Time Out

Experiment with following the broad-S and tight-S eye patterns in these two examples. Notice that the S pattern tends to make indentations on the right and left sides of the line even more extended. The S pattern also tends to make the number of chunks per line (triple, double, or single) more fluid, with some lines taking more soft-focus points than others. In this way, the S pattern can be considered the most organic of speed-reading patterns, in that it adjusts and adapts more naturally to the material being read compared with more formal patterns.

Relax your perceptual powers and "shoulds" regarding reading, say your target affirmation ("Speed up!"), and then let your eyes follow the approximate S pattern in the following examples. Don't give up on this technique if it doesn't seem to work for you at first. Reread both examples several times to reinforce the S pattern for your eyes and mind.

If the S pattern feels promising for your use, apply it to at least ten pages of light and entertaining reading.

Use your pen/pacer to follow along the reverse-S line as you read the following material. Notice that, as in the Z pattern, you will be using your chunking technique on every other line. To help train your eyes to track in the reverse-S pattern, repeat this reading exercise several times.

J. Stacy Adams is the father of equity theories of motivation. Inevitably, he says, we compare what we do and receive with what others do and receive. If we feel an inequity as a result of that comparison, that response can become a powerful factor in determining our own motivational levels. As in the case of Peggy Woodward, few other traditional motivators—salary, reputation, meaningful work—can overcome the deep burn that we feel because of perceived inequity. Adams' way of expressing the relationship between work and equity is as follows: My reward, in consideration of my input, should equal your reward, in consideration of your input. When the sides of this equation are in balance, we feel satisfied and proceed to respond to our usual set of motivators. But when the balance tilts against us, we often act out our frustration and sense of injustice. We may find ourselves acting in several ways in an effort to restore the equity balance. First, we may decide to reduce our input (our effort, involvement, leadership) to produce what we consider a more equitable effort/reward ratio in comparison to others and perhaps to "pay back" those who caused the inequity in the first place. Second, we may try to make the effort/ reward ratio more just by increasing the reward portion. For example, we may ask for an increased salary, a better commission schedule, or a bonus in the form of money or privileges. If we have success at neither of these balancing attempts, we may decide to wipe the board clean entirely by quitting. This action effectively takes us out of what we perceive as an inequitable comparison with others. We may also feel our resignation pays back those who cause the inequity; for a period of weeks or longer, they may have trouble filling our former spot. We imagine that they regret their inequitable action. Third, we can attempt to reestablish an equitable balance between ourselves and others by changing their side of the equation. We could insist, for example, that the other person work harder or receive less money. Fourth, we can attempt to substitute another ratio for the one we dislike. Instead of comparing ourselves disadvantageously to Person A in the company, we may switch our perspective entirely and begin comparing ourselves to Person B.

SUMMING UP

Triple chunking involves three soft-focus points per line, guided by your pacer. These three focus points force your peripheral vision to grasp words in packages, or chunks. The technique of target affirmation—the reminder to "Speed up!" at the beginning of each paragraph—serves to keep the sustained activity of reading from bogging down (with the possible return of old, unproductive reading habits). Double and single chunking, again as guided by your pacer, requires peripheral vision to take in a half or an entire line of print at once. The Z pattern uses chunking to read one line from left to right and then sweeps diagonally across the following line (seeing it in peripheral vision) to read the third line again using the chunking technique. The reverse-S technique allows the Z pattern to be adjusted and adapted to various difficulty levels of prose.

PRACTICE SESSION 7

Use the techniques taught in this chapter to read the following passage. As always, use your pen to pace the movement of your eyes through the lines. Then take the comprehension quiz to gauge in a general way your success in understanding what you have read. If you do well on the quiz, move on to the next practice session. If you do not do well, repeat the reading exercise to make sure you can locate the correct answers. After you have read both reading selections and have taken the comprehension quizzes, reread the passages more quickly by moving your pen at a faster rhythm and making a conscious (but relaxed) effort to practice soft-focus perception of "chunks" of words, not individual letters or words.

TEST SELECTION
Nuns Rule!

Interested in living an extra twenty years—not with magic pills for only $29.50 but with the scientific truth? Learn about an experiment with 700 retired nuns and what a scientist at the University of Kentucky has discovered about longevity.

There is an ongoing experiment with a group of Roman Catholic nuns that ends only with their own autopsies. This genetic research is scheduled to run for decades, and has already produced positive results.

Neurogenesis

Every research project has a theory, and this one, by Dr. David Snowdon of the Sander-Brown Center on Aging at the University of Kentucky, is called neurogenesis—based on the idea that the human brain is capable of growth and regeneration throughout life and into advanced old age. Please note that the average age of the 700 participants is eighty-five years.

Two conclusions have already been substantiated: that active learning is a strategy that can continue throughout life to improve memory and that using your mind for complex thinking reduces the odds of getting Alzheimer's by a minimum of 33 percent. Education level ranges from the bare minimum to university, and careers vary from cook to housekeeper and, in some cases, teachers.

Statistics That Sparkle

Dr. Snowdon directed this project and confirmed that the sisters live at least 25 percent longer than a control group of nuns and remain mentally healthy throughout their long lives. The control group did not pursue active mental activities. The 700 nuns in Mankato, Minnesota actively challenged their brain by training themselves in new hobbies and taking educational courses, year after year. This study is attempting to answer the question whether there is a correlation between actively engaging the mind in cognitive work and long life and mental health.

Neuroplasticity

We all have about 100 billion neurons (nerve cells), which connect to other neurons to create neural network circuitry, based on activity and life experience. The more we use our mind to analyze and learn during our lifetime, the greater the modification of the structure and function of the brain. Consider our brain as the hardware and our experiences, through input, the software (programming).

Active and interactive mental activity on a daily, weekly, and monthly basis causes neuroplasticity—enhancement of our mental power. Usage equals improvement. This is a new scientific principle; prior to the 1990s, the brain was considered fixed in childhood for both structure and function. The prevailing medical view was that millions of neurons die through aging and are not replaced.

Brain Imaging

PET scans, MRIs, and MEG imagery have been used in scientific brain research since the 1990s. They produced conclusive evidence of neurogenesis—the reproduction of new nervous system cells. They prove that our neurons are not hardwired but continue to grow with new experiences. It is now accepted scientifically that the brain can modify itself on the basis of its requirements. Injury or disease may cause loss of neurocircuitry in addition to the aging process. The brain can modify its structure and function to improve its abilities.

When we learn and experience, new synaptic connections are made, the result being new neural networks—regardless of age. Dr. Donald Hebb coined the expression, "the neurons that fire together wire together!" We are capable of changing and modifying our brain circuitry for usefulness through mental exercise. The brain imagery (scans) indicates new dendrite growth on the existing neurons. Learning creates millions of new synaptic connections and firings, together with additional neurotransmitters—chemicals that change brain function.

Mental Firewall

Present research confirms that lifelong learning and experiencing appear to produce a "firewall" in our brain that protects us from Alzheimer's and other brain diseases. Neuroplasticity is the ability of the brain to reprogram areas to overcome injury and disease.

The sisters in Mankato, Minnesota have on file their MRI and other brain scans for annual comparison with the control group. The difference between the two in daily activities is in the use of their minds for learning. Many of the 700 nuns are engaged in teaching and self-improvement. Some are studying for advanced degrees, engaged in learning for learning's sake, and play games that require mental analysis, such as chess and bridge, and some watch *Jeopardy*. Many watch the Discovery Channel and take notes on new discoveries. They read books, journals, and magazines on a daily basis; they enter tournaments and contests requiring advanced skills. They read and analyze the Bible and its commentaries and have discussion groups on their personal interpretations.

End Words

Dr. Yaakov Sterm, professor of neuropsychology at Columbia University in New York City, confirms that college graduates who use their minds for continued learning after retirement significantly stay free of the effects of senility, dementia, depression, and Alzheimer's. He attributes good health in advanced years to a deep supply of neuronal connections in the brain acting as a safety net—a firewall. We suggest the reader use it—not lose it.

Questions for Practice Session 7

1. How would you describe neurogenesis in five words or less?

2. What minimum percentage did the nuns reduce the odds of Alzheimer's? *33%*

3. All of the sisters were physicians. (<u>True</u> or <u>False</u>) All of the sisters were cooks. (True or <u>False</u>)

4. When does the experiment terminate? *death*

5. What university sponsors and monitors the nuns' project? *U of K*

6. During the 1990s, did brain specialists accept the principle of neuroplasticity? (Yes or <u>No</u>). Did they accept neurogenesis? (Yes or <u>No</u>)

7. Name one of the three methods of brain imaging? *MEG, MRI*

8. What is the city and state where the sisters reside? *Mankato Min*

9. How many sisters were included in the research project on aging? *700*

10. Name two playing strategies that helped improve their brain health? ~~mag, games~~ *Discovery Channel, mag, chess*

Answers for Practice Session 7

1. Brain growth or nerve-cell growth.

2. 33 percent.

3. False; false.

4. On death.

5. University of Kentucky.

6. No; no.

7. PET, MRI, or MEG.

8. Mankato, Minnesota.

9. 700.

10. Any two of the following: bridge, chess, watching the Discovery Channel, watching *Jeopardy*, teaching, studying for advanced university degrees.

PRACTICE SESSION 8

Use the techniques taught in this chapter to read the following passage. As always, use your pen to pace the movement of your eyes through the lines. Then take the comprehension quiz to gauge in a general way your success in understanding what you have read. If you do well on the quiz, move on to the next chapter. If you do not do well, repeat the reading exercise to make sure you can locate the correct answers.

After you have read both reading selections and have taken the comprehension quizzes, reread the passages more quickly by moving your pen at a faster rhythm and making a conscious (but relaxed) effort to practice soft-focus perception of "chunks" of words, not individual letters or words.

TEST SELECTION
Blueberries and Mind over Matter

Only fools or con artists claim that adding a particular food to our diet could actually prevent or cure the Big Three—heart disease, cancer, and stroke. Make way for science to reverse that principle. Dr. Barbara Shukill-Hall, of Tufts University in Boston, produced substantial evidence that a delicious half cup of blueberries is our firewall. Further, she says, you can start this regimen past the age of sixty-five and still obtain powerful results, including—get this—a reduction in the standard signs of aging.

She started the experiments with our fellow mammals, the rats, who demanded a dash of sour cream with their less-than-favorite fruit. Elderly rats were fed the equivalent of a half-cup of blueberries daily and showed statistically significant improvement In balance, coordination, and short-term memory. Yes, there are protocols to test the memories of rats, whereby they got extra pellets for successful remembering.

It appears that blueberries have one of the highest concentrations of antioxidants, a proven health preventative, in much higher percentages than in strawberries and spinach. Updated research does in fact indicate that blueberries protect against oxidative stress, which is a proven force in early aging.

The magic lies in the subduing of molecules called oxygen-free radicals, which naturally occur when healthy cells convert oxygen into energy. In acceptable amounts, these bodily free radicals are good guys, ridding the body of toxins, naturally occurring poisons, but in higher levels, free radicals cause serious injury to our DNA and cell membranes. High levels of free radicals permit the viruses and imbalances that cause cancer and heart disease to do their work of illness and death.

In the original rat experiments where rats were fed the essence of blueberry molecules, the effects of aging reversed by almost one-third, and coordination improved dramatically. No, the rats did not qualify for the Athens Olympics, but they added dexterity in negotiating mazes and walking rat trapezes. Extended tests of memory showed improvement beyond the norm in both short- and long-term memory processing.

Among humans, motor behavior loss is the first sign of ordinary aging, and the deterioration continues with the decades. Those who regularly ate a half cup of blueberries maintained their physical dexterity into advanced years.

Now consider this research: A failed experiment to improve the blood flow to the heart to relieve unremitting cardiac pain resulted in up to a 75 percent reduction in such pain.

Ischemic heart disease results from a reduced blood flow to the cardiac muscle and is the precursor to a heart attack. One hundred and eighty-two patients with the highest levels of "intractable angina pain" were part of an experimental surgery that consisted of a laser drilling holes in the wall of the heart muscle. The goal was to create a new channel so that blood within the cavity would detour through the arteries.

It seemed like a good idea at the time, and this special surgery was approved by the experts because neither drugs nor any other form of intervention relieved the intense daily pain of these patients.

One year later none of the patients who were regularly examined showed any increase in blood flow. The experimental laser surgery totally failed to accomplish its goal. Consultations with the patients who had holes drilled in their heart muscles did however report peculiar symptoms. More than 50 percent state they never felt better, all cardiac pain had disappeared, and they were functioning better than ever.

Another large percentage admitted to significant improvement, the pain was materially reduced, and they could now go about their business.

The *Lancet* published the results by Dr. James W. Jones of the University of Missouri. Half the patients reduced their reliance on nitro-glycerin, some halved the number of daily pills taken. Others, who previously could not walk without suffering an instant heart attack, were mobile and moderately active. Many returned to full-time employment and recreational world travel.

Later examination on the treadmill indicated a majority could exercise sixty-five seconds longer than prior to the operation. Control groups showed no significant improvement using drugs alone.

Was it "mind over matter"? Did something physical happen to the cardiac muscles as a result of the laser drilling that was not recorded? The patients continue to be pain free.

Questions for Practice Session 8

1. Which university conducted the blueberry experiments? Tufts

2. The regimen of a half cup of blueberries daily did not work for those of what age? All Ages

3. How were the rats rewarded for successful memory? extra pellets

4. Successful rat experience with blueberries is not transfer-able to humans because of the difference in size and life span. True or <u>false?</u>

5. What substances in blueberries have health-inducing properties? Antioxidents

6. What percentage of pain reduction was experienced by half the patients? 75%

7. The experimental laser surgery was a success in reducing the blood flow. True or false?

8. What medical journal published the heart surgery research?

9. What is the name of the scientist from the University of Missouri who supervised the heart surgery experiment?

10. What was the possible cause of the cardiac pain reduction? ~~laser~~ Mind over matter

Answers for Practice Session 8

1. Tufts University.

2. It worked for all ages.

3. Pellets.

4. False.

5. Antioxidants.

6. 75 percent.

7. False.

8. *Lancet.*

9. Dr. James W. Jones.

10. Mind over matter.

PRACTICE SESSION 9

In the following series of messages, assume that your friends have sent you a flurry of tweets. You haven't had time to respond to each in turn, but instead are reading them for the first time as a series, to which your friends expect a response. Use the eye movement techniques described in this chapter to read through the tweets as quickly as comfort allows. Push yourself to read more quickly than you usually do when reading such messages in real life.

TEST SELECTION
Making Sense of Tweets

"Is the party at 9 or 10 tonight?" Judy

"Ten I think but check with Alice. She's kind of planning it with Alex." Foster

"Why so late?" Judy

"Since when is 10 too late to begin a party. This isn't high school, Judy." Barbara

"Duh. For some of us it's a work day the next day." Judy

"Yeah, me too. Ten is late if it means we're going to be there until 3 A.M. or 4 A.M." Bill

"So do we have anything to say about this? Like, is it cast in granite or something that it starts at 10?" Ralph

"Look, no one is even sure it starts at 10. I said to check with Alice." Foster

"Why Alice?" Judy

"I told you." Foster

"Told me what?" Judy

"Why to check with Alice." Foster

"Is it her party?" Alex

"So let's just ask Alice to start at 8 or 9 instead of 10." Bill

"No one said Alice was in charge of this party." Foster

"Well, I'm not going to get there until 10. Being the first one at a party is just wrong." Barbara

Questions for Practice Session 9

1. Who is the host of this party?

2. What is the earliest time at which at least one of the friends wants the party to start? *8*

3. What is one objection to the party starting at 10 P.M.? *leave la*

4. What is Alice's role in the party?

5. What is the relation between Alex and Alice?

6. How late do some of the partygoers think the party will last? *4*

7. Why has Barbara decided not to show up for the party until 10 P.M.? *1st one is wrong*

8. Who begins the questions about the start time for the party and appears most often in the questions that follow?

Answers for Practice Session 9

1. We don't know for sure.

2. 8 P.M.

3. For some of the partygoers, the next day is a work day.

4. She is helping to plan it.

5. Both are helping to plan the party.

6. 4 A.M.

7. She says she feels it is just wrong.

8. Judy.

Free Reading

For thirty minutes or more, apply the techniques of triple chunking and target affirmation to reading material of your choice. Then, in a separate thirty-minute session, experiment with the double- or single-chunking techniques, as well as the Z and S patterns of eye movement. When you locate a pattern that works well for you, practice it often in your daily reading.

Chapter 6

Understanding and Remembering What You Read

◆

"Beware of dissipating your powers; strive constantly to concentrate them."

—*Goethe (1749–1832)*

THIS CHAPTER ANSWERS FOUR QUESTIONS:

◆ How is it possible that we become aware of much that we have not purposely directed our attention toward?

◆ Why is comprehension most thorough and long lasting when it is based on a holistic view rather than on an attempt to grasp a sequential series of items?

◆ Why should speed-readers set aside the goal of comprehension during the period that they are retraining their eyes and mind to perceive words in new ways?

◆ What is the Fistnotes aid, and how can it improve comprehension, analysis, and memory?

Those who observe speed-readers at work (but have not tried speed-reading themselves) often level the charge that speed-readers "aren't really understanding what they are reading. There's no way they could when they turn pages so quickly!"

This chapter addresses the issue of comprehension—what it is, how it can be achieved, and what interferes with it. To begin this inquiry, please try this brief experiment:

Look out of any window for thirty seconds or so. There is no agenda or "hit list" for your viewing. Simply look out the window and let your eyes and mind travel where they will.

Now answer (to yourself) the following questions:

◆ Did anything in particular attract your attention? If so, what? Why?

◆ What aspects of your view would you consider familiar or expected? Did you tend to focus on them or ignore them?

◆ Did your thoughts actually stay with what you were looking at for the full thirty seconds, or did your mind tend to wander to other priorities and interests having nothing to do with the view?

The thoughts and sensations you experienced looking out the window are in many ways a miniature version of the speed-reading experience. From our earliest school years on, most of us have been educated (or miseducated) to think of a sentence, paragraph, page, chapter, or entire book as a train of sorts, with the first word (like a locomotive) pulling the next word, and so forth, in long, linear string. Our apparent task, as readers, was to observe how car A related to car B, car B to car C, car C to car D, and so forth, to the final caboose ("The End" in a novel).

"Reading carefully," our teachers solemnly told us, means "remembering what we read and being able to discuss and answer questions based on our reading." We learned to test ourselves, by constantly checking our powers of memory; we focused on memorizing the whole "train" as it grew, car by car, before our eyes. This approach to reading yielded at least three results:

◆ It made us read slowly to make sure we "got" (that is, committed to memory) what we had read.

◆ It made us read narrowly, with attention to details (of the sort that we might be quizzed on) rather than larger ideas or perspectives.

◆ It made us think of much of our reading as a difficult, frustrating activity that "tested" us (and often left us feeling dumb).

A NEW VIEW OF COMPREHENSION AND MEMORY

We cannot pour the old wine of traditional reading and trivia-oriented comprehension into the new bottles of speed-reading. Specifically, we cannot retrain the eyes and mind to new patterns of perception while simultaneously asking the old questions, "But can you list in order the points you have just read, using the same key words as the writer?" To become a speed-reader and end up comprehending and remembering much more of what you read, it's absolutely necessary in the first stages of learning to relax an obsessive concern: "Am I getting everything?"

When you looked out the window in the experiment that opened this chapter, did you "get everything"? Of course not. Among the hundreds (and, in reality, thousands upon thousands) of items you were able to see in any typical view out the window, you focused on certain things and demoted other observable things to "background" or "unconscious" levels. (Interestingly, under hypnosis you can be made to recall many of these items that you saw but did not elevate to conscious attention.)

At first, speed-reading will resemble a look out the window. Certainly you will think that you're "getting something"— that is, focusing on some aspects of your reading—but you will also have the strong sensation that you're not going to be able to reproduce or memorize everything that appears before you. In fact, in the act of reading, you are scanning a landscape (looking out a window) more than focusing, one by one, on train cars passing in sequence before your eyes and mind.

With practice, using the techniques taught in these chapters, you will gain confidence, and you will "get" the landscape view more and more completely. In other words, you will develop the ability to see details in context. Just as your eye sweeps by many aspects of the look out the window as unremarkable "background," so your eyes and mind learn to sweep by word images and ideas according to their relative importance to the whole picture emerging before you. Like an art expert who knows what to look for in a particular painting, you end up able to answer comprehension and memory questions far better than the amateur who tries to examine the painting by counting its birds, listing its trees, and enumerating how many different colors were used (in other words, taking the sequential, or train-car, approach to perception and understanding).

INCREASING YOUR MASTERY OF COMPREHENSION AND MEMORY

Therefore, it is the usual experience of successful speed-readers that their ability to comprehend and remember grows steadily with their reading speed. They realize that, at first, their eyes and mind will not be used to employing the powerful resource of peripheral vision to gather information—and that comprehension may initially suffer as a result. However, that early downturn in comprehension versus the snail-paced reading approach is a small and temporary price to pay for the long-term benefits of reading three or four times faster and comprehending more than ever before.

In addition to this natural upward trend for comprehension and memory as part of the speed-reading experience, a special tool—Fistnotes—can aid you in "thinking with" the writer (and often a step ahead of him or her). This tool is a powerful aid to understanding in the same way that the techniques contained in these chapters are a reliable route to speed-reading. Here's how Fistnotes works:

As you read, imagine a hand collecting the most important aspects of what you are reading. Each digit on the hand plus the palm of the hand play a role in gathering impressions and ideas that add up to 90 percent in more thorough understanding and 50 percent in reliable long-term memory. The Fistnotes aid can be visualized as follows:

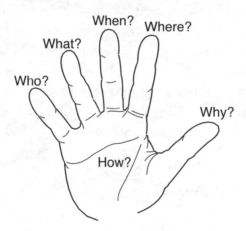

Each digit represents a question you will ask in the act of reading—and an answer you will have "in the palm of your hand," so to speak, once you've come upon it in your reading.

These questions, by the way, are the same classic queries used by reporters in gathering the basic facts of any story:

◆ Who? (little finger)

◆ What? (ring finger)

◆ When? (middle finger)

◆ Where? (pointer finger)

◆ Why? (thumb)

◆ How? (palm of the hand)

Robert Louis Stevenson called these questions "my six friends who taught me everything I know."

The Fistnote aid can be used to "fill out the picture" as you read. Sometimes you discover that the writer or speaker has left out some aspect of the "5 W's and 1 H"—for example, a report that fails to specify "Why?" in discussing a business problem. In this case you have not simply followed and remembered the writer's presentation of ideas. You have also analyzed it (that is, evaluated it) and found it lacking in crucial ways.

USING THE FISTNOTES AID

You will be glad to know you won't be writing anything down in the process of using Fistnotes. Simply tuck a finger or thumb toward your palm as soon as you've answered the question it represents. You'll end up with a fist that wraps up the aspects that matter most for the topic you've been reading about.

Let's imagine that you're reading a report on options for child care at your company. The author of the report has no obligation to answer your Who? What? When? Where? Why? How? questions in that particular order. You must be ready, therefore, to take note of his or her points in the order they occur. For argument's sake, we will say that the main points of the report occur as follows:

(little finger) Who? (40 percent of employees with preschool-aged children have signed a petition to management requesting consideration of child-care benefits during the workday.)

(ring finger) What? (These employees aren't sure whether they want an on-site child-care center or vouchers that can be used in child-care centers within their neighborhoods.)

(middle finger) When? (The petition was delivered last week. The employees request a meeting with management within thirty days and action on their request within three months.)

(pointer finger) Where? (On-site child care would require an initial investment by the company but would prove less expensive than vouchers in the long term.)

(thumb) Why? (The employees list two main reasons for company-sponsored child care: 1. absenteeism to breakdowns in child-care arrangements is costing the company $200,000 per year; 2. company-sponsored child care will help attract new employees.)

(palm) How? (Employees suggest that an experienced child-care consultant be retained to advise the companies and its employees of the various options and best practices available.)

In this way, the Fistnotes memory aid helps you organize a series of related ideas based on what you have. By quickly reviewing the points "at the tips of your fingers," you can discuss the report intelligently and recall its major assertions.

Once you have the gist of information in the document, you will find that you are able to speed-read with greater ease and confidence. After all, many (if not most) business documents are filled with redundancy, irrelevant points, and other forms of filler. Your use of Fistnotes has helped you cut to the chase of the main argument in the document. You've put yourself in a good position to quickly recognize what's germane to the issue at hand and what's just fluff.

Time Out

Select some document from your professional life. Read it using your pacer, indentation, and other speed-reading techniques—but this time with the Fistnotes aid at work. After one reading, check each of the digits on your hand as well as your palm to see if you have grasped (and can name) the major points of the document. If so, congratulate yourself and resolve to use the Fistnotes technique frequently in your work-related reading. If not, read the document one more time (without sacrificing speed) to see if any additional ideas become clear. After this review, decide whether you missed essential ideas in your reading or (as is often the case) the author neglected to include these ideas in the first place.

SUMMING UP

Just as the eyes are able to take in (through peripheral vision) more than they see in hard focus, so the mind is able to comprehend images, impressions, ideas, and other information that lie outside a person's specific purposeful concentration. Learning to tap the outlying regions of "peripheral comprehension" allows a speed-reader to develop faster and faster patterns of eye movement across the page without sacrificing comprehension. The Fistnotes technique provides a handy (pardon the pun) way of keeping track of who, what, when, where, why, and how as one reads. The technique is especially useful in analyzing what may be missing in a writer's argument and for recalling core elements of a reading selection.

Free Reading

Choose reading material that is somewhat more difficult than the material you have used for past Free Reading assignments. Use the Fistnotes technique to keep track of core ideas as you read. When you have completed your reading, try to sum up aloud the 5 W's and 1 H of the Fistnotes pattern.

Appendix A

Making Speed-Reading a Company Value and Advantage

Thus far we have presented speed-reading as an individual challenge and opportunity. We have argued for at least four professional advantages that stem from even modest progress in speed-reading:

◆ The employee reads more—a crucial advantage at a time when career advancement depends upon creativity, innovation, and new knowledge.

◆ The employee remembers more—an enhancement to his or her status as a contributing team member, especially in briefings, meetings, and interviews.

◆ The employee balances work and personal life more successfully, since reading tasks from work do not encroach on personal time, home life, and rest/restoration time.

◆ The employee is able to respond to change and get "up to speed" more quickly, thanks to his or her ability to read quickly and comprehend thoroughly.

There is no reason why these advantages cannot be attained for larger employee groups, divisions, or entire workforces. Typically such work is undertaken by training departments within organizations. To aid their efforts, this Appendix presents a model syllabus for presenting a corporate speed-reading course using this book. This model syllabus assumes four half-day meetings, but of course these lesson divisions can be altered to meet a company's specific needs and scheduling limitations. For example, a company could choose to present this material in three full-day sessions or eight two-hour sessions. In any of these cases, it is recommended that two days or more be provided between sessions so that participants have a chance to practice their newly learned skills on their own.

SYLLABUS

Corporate Speed-Reading

Six half-day sessions

Recommended: One half-day session per week for six consecutive weeks

Required textbook: *Ultimate Speed-Reading*

Session 1 Prereading Chapters 1–3
    First two hours: "Let's make a list and then analyze and discuss specifically what goes wrong in our company owing to poor reading practices."
    Second two hours: "Let's learn the underlining technique and practice it using our pacers."

Session 2 Prereading Chapter 4
    First two hours: "Let's understand the indentation process and then practice it on a variety of business reading materials."
    Second two hours: "Let's understand the importance of using peripheral vision through soft focus and then practice this technique."

Session 3 Prereading Chapter 5

First two hours: "Let's understand the triple-chunking process and then apply it to our business reading."

Second two hours: "Let's learn how to use target affirmation, the Z pattern, and the reverse-S pattern to raise reading rates to even higher levels."

Session 4 Prereading Chapter 6

First two hours: "Let's put the whole package together by practicing all the speed-reading skills we have learned and then taking a few comprehension measurements to make sure we are understanding what we are reading."

Second two hours: "Let's discuss and come up with an action plan for how speed-reading can become a vital part of company culture and practices. What advantages can we gain from our newfound skill in speed-reading and improved comprehension?

Readings and Resources

◆

RECOMMENDED BOOKS ON SPEED-READING

Buzan, Tony. *Speed Reading*. Plume Books, 1991.

Cisek, Jan. *Spd Rdng—The Speed Reading Bible*. Saffire Press, 2012.

Cutler, Wade. *Triple Your Reading Speed*. 4th ed. Pocket Press, 2003.

Ford, Michael. *Speed Reader X: Speed Reading Made Easy*. Elite Minds, Inc., 2005.

Frank, Stanley. *Remember Everything You Read: The Evelyn Wood 7-Day Speed Reading and Learning Program*. Avon, 1992.

Kump, Peter. *Breakthrough Rapid Reading*. Prentice Hall, 1998.

Marks-Beale, Abby, et al. *The Complete Idiot's Guide to Speed Reading*. Alpha, 2008.

Moidel, Steve. *Speed Reading for Business*. 2nd ed. Barron's Educational Series, Inc., 1998.

Ostrov, Rick. *Power Reading: The Best, Fastest, Easiest, Most Effective Course on Speedreading and Comprehension Ever Developed!* Education Press, 2001.

Smith, Nila Banton. *Speed Reading Made Easy.* Warner Books, 1987.

Spargo, Edward. *Timed Readings: Fifty 400-Word Passages with Questions for Building Reading Speed.* 3rd ed. McGraw-Hill, 1989.

Zorn, Robert L. *Speed Reading.* HarperTorch, 1995.

AUDIO CASSETTES

Fritsch, Edward L. *Master Reader: The 4-Hour Speed-Reading, Speed-Thinking Course.* Coach Series, 2005.

Scheele, Paul R. *Double Your Reading Speed in 10 Minutes.* Learning Strategies Corporation, 1999.

INTERNET SITES

ARC speed-reading plus. *www.advancedreading.com*

Learn speed-reading. *www.SpeedReadingTactics.com*

Speed-reading and memory training for Windows. *www.rocketreader.com*

Speed-reading self-pacing methods. *www.english.glendale. cc.ca.us/methods.html*

Speed-reading software. *www.acereader.com*

Speed-reading test online. *www.readingsoft.com*

Suggestions for improving reading speed. *www.ucc.vt.edu/stdysk/suggest.html*

TurboRead speed-reading. *www.turboread.com*

INDEX

BARRON'S

Paving your way to business success

Barron's Business Success Guides

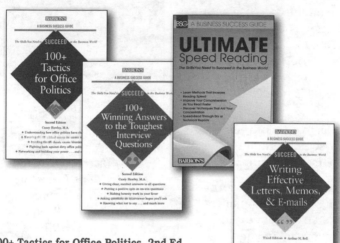

100+ Tactics for Office Politics, 2nd Ed.
ISBN: 978-0-7641-3913-0, $8.99, *Can$10.99*

100+ Winning Answers to the Toughest Interview Questions, 2nd Ed.
ISBN: 978-0-7641-3912-3, $8.99, *Can$10.99*

Ultimate Speed Reading
ISBN: 978-1-4380-0165-4, $8.99, *Can$9.99*

Writing Effective Letters, Memos, & E-mails, 3rd Ed.
ISBN: 978-0-7641-2453-2. $8.95, *Can$10.99*

Available at your local book store
or visit **www.barronseduc.com**

(#73a) R 11/12

Barron's Educational Series, Inc.
250 Wireless Blvd.
Hauppauge, N.Y. 11788
Order toll-free: 1-800-645-3476
Order by fax: 1-631-434-3217

In Canada:
Georgetown Book Warehouse
34 Armstrong Ave.
Georgetown, Ontario L7G 4R9
Canadian orders: 1-800-247-7160
Order by fax: 1-800-887-1594

Prices subject to change
without notice.

Sound Advice for the Experienced Investor

Licensed investment advisor and best-selling author Phil DeMuth addresses the issues facing one of the most overlooked segments of the equities investment community—those with portfolios worth more than $100,000. In this in-depth guide, DeMuth offers the more experienced investor the tools needed to—

- Custom tailor their asset allocation to their personal circumstances

- Recognize outperforming market anomalies and use them to gain increased income

- Keep what they've got and avoid what he calls "Wall Street's wealth extraction machine"

Here are investment strategies for the affluent—and those who are approaching affluence and trying to take that big step forward.

The Affluent Investor: Financial Advice to Grow and Protect Your Wealth

Phil DeMuth, Ph.D. with an Introduction by Ben Stein

Hardcover w/jacket, 6" x 9"
ISBN: 978-0-7641-6564-1
$22.99, Can$26.50

Available at your local book store or visit **www.barronseduc.com**

Barron's Educational Series, Inc.
250 Wireless Blvd.
Hauppauge, NY 11788
Order toll-free: 1-800-645-3476

Prices subject to change without notice.

In Canada:
Georgetown Book Warehouse
34 Armstrong Ave.
Georgetown, Ont. L7G 4R9
Canadian orders: 1-800-247-7160

(#273) R1/13